Internal Family Systems

Internal Family Systems

Making a Start (and Getting Curious)

EMMA E. REDFERN

sheldon PRESS

First published in Great Britain by Sheldon Press in 2026
An imprint of John Murray Press

1

Copyright © Emma E. Redfern 2026

The right of Emma E. Redfern to be identified as the Author of the Work
has been asserted by her in accordance with the Copyright, Designs and
Patents Act 1988.

This book is for information or educational purposes only and is not intended
to act as a substitute for medical advice or treatment. Any person with a
condition requiring medical attention should consult a qualified medical
practitioner or suitable therapist.

A CIP catalogue record for this title is available from the British Library

Trade Paperback ISBN 978 1 399 82294 7
ebook ISBN 978 1 399 82295 4

Typeset by KnowledgeWorks Global Ltd.

Printed and bound in Great Britain by Clays Ltd, Elcograf S.p.A.

John Murray Press policy is to use papers that are natural, renewable and
recyclable products and made from wood grown in sustainable forests.
The logging and manufacturing processes are expected to conform to the
environmental regulations of the country of origin.

John Murray Press
Carmelite House
50 Victoria Embankment
London EC4Y 0DZ

www.sheldonpress.co.uk

John Murray Press, part of Hodder & Stoughton Limited
An Hachette UK company

The authorised representative in the EEA is Hachette Ireland, 8 Castlecourt Centre,
Dublin 15, D15 XTP3, Ireland (email: info@hbgi.ie)

Contents

Journal prompts

Introduction

Welcome, dear reader. I'm hoping that you may have been drawn to this book partly because of the beautiful cover depicting a glimpse beneath the ocean. It shows sunbursts and shadows together with the suggestion of the sea creatures and other wondrous and curious things living beneath the ocean surface from the shallows to its depths. My hope is that, as you engage with this book, it will take you on a journey beneath your surface to explore your own inner ecosystem.

I'm curious: how do you enter the sea? Are you like me, inching in, squealing as I go? Or perhaps your style is similar to my husband's? He wades to a certain level then plunges under the surface. Perhaps you like to dive gracefully from a height, or maybe paddling is your preference? Whatever your style as you enter this book, may you find something to free your inner curiosity. Unlike my tentative style of sea entry, I'm just going to dive into the Introduction. Let's get started!

IFS and mental health and well-being

This book offers an introduction to how an understanding of Internal Family Systems (IFS for short) can improve mental health and well-being. Currently sweeping the globe as a form of psychotherapy, IFS also offers more than that: as a 'practice for life', it provides constructive ways of understanding ourselves which can contribute to a compassionate, connected and, above all, curious way of living with ourselves and others. Additionally, many consider it a spiritual practice or spiritual homecoming. As you read further, I ask you to keep an open mind, a beginner's mind, and decide for yourself if and how IFS will feature in your life.

So, what is mental health? According to the World Health Organization, it is a state of mental well-being that enables people to cope with the stresses of life, realize their abilities, learn well and work well, and contribute to their community ... [It] underpins our individual and collective abilities to make decisions, build relationships and shape the world we live in. Mental health is a basic human right.[1]

And yet, according to the UK's National Audit Office (NAO), in 2021–22, the National Health Service spent only around 8 per cent of its total budget on mental health services in England.[2] Without letting our governments off the hook, it is vital that individuals and groups (professional and otherwise) continue to find ways of managing and improving our mental health and helping others to do the same. I consider using the Internal Family Systems model to be one such way.

IFS works on the premise that people are 'multi-minded' or have many minds, each one belonging to an inner subpersonality – what IFS calls a 'part'. These parts make up one's inner family. In IFS, not just every person, but every *part* of every person has the right to mental health.

Experiencing IFS can be profoundly transformative as it helps each of us access our own inner state of health and well-being, the essence of each of us that IFS calls our Self, with which all parts of us can connect. In this book, you will be reading about Self, the inner liberator, healer and leader, one of whose essential qualities is curiosity. This inner 'Self with a capital S' is a tremendous protective factor in maintaining or achieving mental health. Self exists in each of us and, beyond IFS, it is known by many names. IFS is the method developed by Richard Schwartz and others over the past 40-plus years to consistently access this inner resource for mental health and well-being.

How about you?

I'm wondering about you, your mental health and well-being. Maybe you are curious about this IFS as featured in podcasts and

YouTube videos. Perhaps you've had therapy before, some of it 'successful' and some of it less so, and want to know more about IFS therapy before giving it a go. Alternatively, you (or someone close to you) might be experiencing some mental health challenges or relationship difficulties that have led you here. Or it might be that you are invested in self-development, searching for a way to feel more whole and authentically you, and more able to cope in a world that feels more awry than you'd like.

No matter what brought you to IFS, this book has much to offer you. Mine is a unique voice and viewpoint; I include portions of my personal story and write about things in ways that others do not. I hope this fresh approach will be invigorating if you are already 'in the know' and enlightening if this is your first IFS book. Although I draw much from my experience with my clients in therapy, any examples not my own or quoted with permission are composite and fictionalized. You may recognize yourself or those close to you in some of them.

My hope is that this introductory guide to the IFS model will ignite a spark of interest in the power of curiosity and its relevance in your own and others' lives. May you experience the transformations possible when you understand and can use some of the concepts and practices of IFS! For you and yours, I wish improved mental health, more ease in becoming emotionally regulated, enhanced relationships, and feeling more at home in and as your whole self.

Moving forward with this book: what's inside

Section 1 introduces key IFS concepts across three chapters. In **Chapter 1** I highlight some of the challenges of being multiple – having parts inside – and I emphasize the importance of appreciating and validating our subpersonalities for their amazing contributions to our lives. Without our parts, we would not function. **Chapter 2** provides standard IFS teaching on the nature of the different categories of parts and their burdens. **Chapter 3** focuses on Self, the inner liberator, healer and leader, and how it relates to self (lowercase 's') and Larger Self.

Section 2 introduces key IFS practices across two chapters. First, **Chapter 4** introduces the idea of getting to know parts and parts getting to know Self inside (Self-to-part relationships). **Chapter 5** outlines the IFS steps of healing used in therapy to meet, unburden and liberate the wounded parts of us.

Section 3 explores how you can use IFS yourself. **Chapter 6** begins to prepare the ground for building and nurturing internal relationships. **Chapter 7** describes various ways to come to meet your parts. **Chapter 8** goes deeper into how IFS can transform thinking about and communicating with oneself and others in everyday life.

Section 4, Troubleshooting, is where to turn if you are struggling to implement any of the exercises mentioned in this book or in other IFS texts – when IFS seems not to be working (**Chapter 9**) or to be working too well (**Chapter 10**). This section identifies some common ways we trip ourselves up and inadvertently block the transformational power of IFS. If you are a trained professional, these two chapters may be of especial interest at moments when a client's system has you stumped.

In three chapters, Section 5 highlights some of the many benefits that come from embracing IFS: truth and freedom (**Chapter 11**); emotional regulation and reduced reactivity (**Chapter 12**); and self-acceptance and authenticity (**Chapter 13**). (Please note that **Chapter 11** begins with an exploration of suicide and **Chapter 2** also references suicidality.)

Section 6 provides appendices, endnotes and references for taking your understanding further as you and your internal family system continue journeying with IFS. One appendix offers a Self-leadership measure, if any of your parts would like to enjoy a 'before and after' self-assessment. (I suggest taking the quiz the first time right after you've read this book, then returning to it again periodically to measure how your system might have evolved over time.) The next appendix briefly introduces adverse childhood experiences (ACEs) and protective factors. The final appendix gives basic hints and tips about taking yourself into IFS therapy (or not).

A gentle caution

Learning about IFS is often so transformative that people's most enthusiastic parts want to tell everyone else all about it, right away. Please help such parts of yourself be mindful about how and when you share what you learn as you read, and with whom. I'm referring to your own process and anything you might notice about someone else! Let tact and discretion, and choosing a good enough time, triumph over enthusiastic haste.

I recommend reading from front to back, as the material builds on itself. However you find it, thank you for being here. May your curiosity be both satisfied and piqued as you find challenge, permission and mirroring. May living with more curiosity bring up from beneath the surface psychological and emotional riches.

What this book is not

This isn't a book driven by symptoms, though I include examples of common ailments and struggles for us humans in the twenty-first century. This book is not intended as a stand-alone solution if you are suffering from severe mental health symptoms or have one or more major diagnoses. It may offer support and assistance, but it is not designed or intended as a cure-all, unfortunately; if only a book had that power, and that I could write it for you to read!

As the title suggests, this is an introduction. It is not a book that will enable you to become an IFS therapist or practitioner, though it will be of use if you are either. An outline of how to progress through all the IFS steps of healing is included, alongside guidance as to how to accompany yourself inside, but there's nothing quite like having an attuned, skilled therapy professional alongside you, present and guiding inner exploration.[3] To go further and deeper, I suggest you avail yourself of someone trained in IFS who is used to taking parts of you who are hurting inside through a full healing journey. Even the founder himself, Richard Schwartz – who goes by 'Dick' – does his deeper inner work accompanied.

No matter how you use it, benefits await those in your internal and external world if you take this book to heart, with curiosity as your guide.

Actively welcoming IFS into your life is becoming curious about yourself (and your Self) as a human doing, being, and continuing to come into being. It invites you on a journey inward towards your wellness and wholeness, towards your wounded ones and those who protect them.

Moving inwards using this book

The book and I offer you an opportunity to look, listen and feel inside: to come to know directly what and who is running daily life, as well as what and who might be locked away out of your awareness. In IFS language, this is called a U-turn or **You-turn**, when you turn inwards to yourself and away from the distractions of other people, problems and tasks.

The You-turn

Named after the manoeuvre in driving whereby a vehicle is driven to turn a U-shaped course, so it faces in the opposite direction. A You-turn is an act of turning away from the outer world and becoming curious towards our own internal world and reactivity. Doing a You-turn is a first step in developing a two-way relationship between our Self and each of our parts.

If you are not comfortable doing a You-turn initially, that's okay, too. This is a book that can be enjoyed at different levels and by different parts of an internal family: the studious ones who like theory, metaphor and case material; the ones who learn by doing, including putting it down on paper; the ones who like to try something in real life, and more.

I ask that you engage with only as much as your system allows at any moment. If your engagement is slight to start with, this might change later, and it would be worth coming back to the book in the future. Because parts' preferences, learning styles and ways of experiencing differ – and your circumstances may not always be the same – there is a variety of material to experience:

- Metaphors galore, case material and reconstructed IFS sessions
- Explanations in shaded boxes of key concepts, which appear in bold type
- Thoughts and words of parts, which appear in italics without quotation marks
- Journal prompts at chapter ends encouraging curiosity
- Examples from my life and those of other IFS professionals
- Summaries and exercises to try for yourself.

Take a risk on yourself; what's the worst that can happen as you engage with the book? Seriously, that's not a bad question to ask – and it's even better if you listen for an answer (or answers).

Taking the risk and ...

Trusting me

Who am I to be writing a book that has been published for you to read? Especially a book of big promises and big asks. Perhaps you have sceptical or doubting parts who wonder if I'm up to the job of introducing you to IFS and guiding your use of aspects of it; what are my credentials? I'm glad you asked!

First, since my initial therapy in 1999 (group psychotherapy as an in- and out-patient, having been diagnosed with post-traumatic stress disorder, PTSD), I've become accustomed to being a client. I believe this brings some sensitivity to my writing about mental health and healing. Also, this means I have some awareness of the challenges and joys of changing both on the inside and in the outside world. As a child, I enjoyed watching Gene Roddenberry's *Star Trek* TV family, who boldly went where no one had gone before in outer space. Now, as an adult, I understand how challenging, risky and rewarding it can be to boldly go where no one has gone before *inside ourselves*. It would be an honour if you would permit me and my inner family to accompany you as you journey with this book and its exercises and information.

Second, I get what it's like to learn how to be curious and caring about myself. Until I had a breakdown/breakthrough experience in my early thirties that led to the therapy I mentioned, a group of intellectual, nice, responsible outward-facing protector parts mostly ran the Emma Redfern show. Curiosity was an intellectual commodity used in service of academic and professional success (of which there was plenty for this first-generation university graduate). Fortunately, and unfortunately, that life crashed and burned, whereupon I discovered psychotherapy as a client, together with the concept of self-care. Curiosity became more than intellectual; it became deeply personal and health-giving to take an interest in myself and my inner workings.

Third, this isn't my first IFS book. As a trained and experienced psychotherapy supervisor, in January 2019 the idea came to me of creating a multi-author book on the supervision and consultation of IFS (Redfern, 2023a). Curiously, the idea for *this* book came to me in January 2016, but it got left behind as I attended to other IFS writing projects (Redfern, 2023b; Foot and Redfern, 2023). Now, ten years later, here it is – although in a very different guise than was originally intended.

Finally, and perhaps most important to any concerned parts or those who've had poor experiences with therapists and helpers, I've been working as a psychotherapist for 23 years and as a supervisor of psychotherapists for 16. Although I'm human and parts of me have made and continue to make mistakes, I firmly believe in the importance of relationship in addition to (or over) a therapy protocol. I seek to bring love to fear, and value safety over speed. I learned relational psychotherapy before I trained in therapies such as IFS which have recognizable protocols or steps; my supervision training was systemic and relational. More and more I value the importance of creating a relationship that is therapeutic, even when using powerful protocol-based methods such as IFS. I urge you to favour having relationships with your parts over 'doing a protocol', though the former may evolve out of the latter.

That said, I want to tell your sceptical parts that I am not a researcher. I have little scientific bent and will be using personal examples from my own life and fictionalized examples from my professional life to illuminate what I write about. For parts who prefer more rigour, I recommend the writings of Richard Schwartz and Martha Sweezy. Also, in the spirit of transparency and trust-building, here is where I let all readers know that this is not an official IFS Institute book. I am pleased and proud to contribute in my own way to the institute's ongoing effort to share IFS with the public.

Trusting IFS

What makes the Internal Family Systems model worth trusting? First, IFS is a pragmatic approach derived directly from what works in therapy. Schwartz, the founder, figurehead and pre-eminent global champion of the model, tells of how, as a family systems therapist in the 1980s, he was running a failing clinical study using his existing approach. Out of desperation and in line with his values, he followed the data his clients were presenting to him. Really listening to what they were sharing about their inner lives, he began applying external family systems therapy interventions to the inner worlds of his clients. From there, the basic theoretical tenets of IFS were discovered, and Schwartz gathered around him trusted psychotherapy professionals to explore those principles and devise practices to apply them efficiently and humanely. The result is now known as the Internal Family Systems model.

Second, IFS is building a base of clinical evidence for its effectiveness. Since IFS became established as one of the hottest tickets in town in terms of transformational psychotherapy, the IFS Institute and its charitable arm, the Foundation of Self Leadership, as well as the Cambridge Mental Health Alliance, have begun to focus on creating clinical trials to establish IFS as an evidence-based practice. If you wish, you can read the published outcomes of the trials so far, which very much suggest that IFS is worth trusting in.[4] In the UK, IFS is becoming popular as a focus for research, for example in the Lancaster University clinical psychology doctoral programme and Sherwood Psychotherapy Training Institute.

Third, IFS is a non-pathologizing approach. IFS teaches that it's helpful *not* to view clients as a medical professional might, through a lens of diagnosing what's wrong with the person and in need of putting right. Rather, like many other therapies, in which the therapist hopes to become unnecessary in time, IFS has built within it the idea that you already have what you need within you to heal and thrive. IFS also acknowledges that you will have many inner (and possibly outer) constraints to that healing and thriving, some of which IFS can equip you to ascertain and address. Unlike Maria in *The Sound of Music*, parts are not problems to be solved.

Fourth, IFS is what's known as a 'transformative' psychotherapy rather than a 'counteractive' one.[5] By transformative, I mean that incorporating IFS into life can have everlasting results which may not need constant reinforcement to maintain their benefits. In terms of counteractive therapy, think cognitive behavioural therapy (CBT), which has an emphasis on countering or opposing existing so-called negative thoughts, feelings and behaviours so you can think, feel and do something more positive or adaptive. While often helpful for day-to-day life, a counteractive approach takes constant effort to maintain, may not get to the roots of an issue, and can heighten inner conflict between parts of yourself. Using IFS as a practice for living, by contrast, can lead to a transformed relationship to and with yourself, one that's more curious, compassionate and open.

Trusting yourself and your Self

I don't know your history, including your experiences in therapy, nor have details of any medication you take for your mental health. I won't know how well or how badly authority figures (parents, teachers, therapists, medical professionals, etc.) have attuned to you, listened to you and then responded to your needs (or not). Nor will I know how badly parts of you feel at letting yourself down; choices made and now regretted; risks never taken that parts of you wish you had. It is possible that you will confront, possibly even heal, some of this past material and experiences as you progress through the book. More importantly, I assure you that it is never too late to learn new ways to relate to yourself and to others.

For now, as an experiment, I'm asking you to entertain a few simple ideas:

- At your core, you have a loving Self who is available to lead your inner family (your inner system) if your parts allow.
- The more accepting and welcoming of parts your system can be, the more transformation will be possible.
- Parts (like people) make mistakes, and they (and you) are more than those mistakes.

- There is no perfection this side of eternity. We are all works in progress and will undoubtedly depart this mortal coil with healing still outstanding.
- The less parts strive and the more they relax, the further your system will journey on the path to inner harmony and balance.

More on all of this to follow.

Journal prompts

Asking inside and listening for answers

Ask inside: What is the worst that can happen as I engage with this book? Then: Listen for any answers you might hear, and write down or in some way record any ensuing dialogue.

Ask inside: What is my intention or hope in reading this book? (You may have more than one hope and intention.) Then: Listen for answers and record any ensuing dialogue.

Ask inside: What do I (or we) need as we read and engage with this book? Then: Listen for answers, write them down or in some way record them. Ask about what needs action, for whom. How might you take those actions to meet those needs?

Section 1
KEY IFS CONCEPTS

1

The many parts of who you are

It's been a while since I dined out alone, and I didn't manage it this morning either. I'd got the café's opening time wrong and after a long walk to reach it, my back was communicating to me not to hang around, so I came home to porridge as usual in my back-friendly chair. I had imagined arriving at the café without my usual friend or husband, and the server asking, 'Just you?' or 'Table for one?' And, of course, the answer would have been, 'Yes, just me' or 'Yes, table for one, please.' After all, I have only one physical me to take up one physical chair.

But my parts (some of whom you'll come to recognize) mischievously, and pedantically, know that it's never 'just one'. I am never just one Emma. In fact, I'd gone out for a walk with parts who were upset with myself and my husband. I wanted to treat me and my inner team, some of whom were in distress, to a breakfast prepared by someone else just for once and eaten with a consciously loving presence: the deeper inner me known as Self.

Parts (and people) are more than they seem
The insides don't match the outsides

There is more than one 'me' inside Emma Redfern, and there is also more than one 'you' inside of you. You might recognize this in everyday decision-making. First thing in the morning I'm aware of the different possibilities for my pre-work time: go for a quick walk before breakfast or revise a Word document I'm sharing with a colleague? *You've got to do your physio exercises too, don't forget,* a voice warns in my head. I'm also aware of the various extra demands to fit around work: put the washing on now or leave it until later? *Better check the weather first,* says someone else inside. Will I have the energy and time to make dinner after work, or do I need to make a start on it now? *You'll be too tired later,* another voice chips in.

Maybe you're not consciously aware of such internal processes, or your routine is more predetermined than mine. But I suspect you'll recognize a similar kind of internal conversation from your own life – it's probably just what you call 'thinking'. The diversity of our thoughts confronts us with a fundamental difficulty facing us as humans: we are simultaneously singular (as our physicality and use of language suggests: 'I', 'me', even 'you' in English) and contain multitudes. When we look in the mirror, we see only one of us, yet we are so much more than can be seen from the outside; like the TARDIS, we are bigger on the inside! This is both advantageous and a drawback.

Although I gave mundane daily examples above, any of which could have been chosen without too much concern, constantly being 'in two minds' (or more), without some ways to respond to this inner division or conflict, leads to inner and relational stress. On the other hand, stalwartly holding on to your 'singularity' or oneness can be just as damaging and problematic – not least because it defies your inner-world reality.

Parts of ourselves who achieve outer-world success can sometimes think they are all there is to who we are. For years, a part of me believed she was the one and only Emma Redfern: the 'together' white girl who aced it at school and later showed up at work, the driven and successful intellectual woman, fulfilling her destiny as 'mother's good/clever girl'.

Mirror, mirror, on the wall, who is the fairest of them all?

Did you notice in the italic text at the start of the chapter – a couple of the phrases began with 'you'? Were you curious about who was speaking and who the 'you' was they were speaking to? By the end of the book, you'll have more awareness of some of the voices inside your system. I gave innocuous examples earlier, but there are times when an inner voice can speak harshly, even mercilessly! For some of us, this occurs when we look in the mirror and don't see the fairest but the ugliest person of all – or so someone on the inside declares.

Inner criticism often happens for us humans, and seems to fly under the radar unless we have therapy, which can help us slow down and notice our inner 'self-talk'. The member of our inner team who is looking through our eyes at any moment will determine what we see, how we judge it, and whether we pass comment on it or not. For example, Western society today has a noticeable bias against people living in larger bodies or defying gender norms. There remains an over-emphasis on certain narrow expectations of what looks 'good' and is 'acceptable'. Children are still largely socialized to belong to and look like one gender not the other, boy or girl. These cultural pressures might show up in a person's inner dialogue thus: *What do you look like? You can't go out in that! If you go out looking like that, you'll get beaten up and it'll be your own fault.*

In June 2024, my professional body, the British Association for Counselling and Psychotherapy (BACP), published details of a survey of 1,000 women in relation to their self-doubt and **self-esteem.** The survey cited body image as the leading source of self-esteem issues for 61 per cent of the women surveyed, with 54 per cent agreeing their self-esteem impacts their day-to-day choices. Worryingly, BACP's research found that self-esteem issues were experienced for the first time at around ten years of age by 10 per cent of the women.[1]

> ## Self-esteem
>
> 'Self-esteem' refers to having confidence in one's own worth or abilities. Similar words would be 'self-respect', 'self-regard' and 'self-confidence'. The word is used in therapy culture by clients and professionals alike as if there were only one 'self' to esteem. For an IFS multiplicity-based alternative, go to **Appendix 1**.

Enjoying multiplicity – variety is the spice of life

I hope that, by the end of the book, your system will feel more appreciated and 'enjoyed' than might be the case at present. But for now, let me suggest that variety is the spice of life! Who doesn't love to be a little mysterious, or to surprise their nearest and dearest by showing a side to their character they mostly keep hidden, or reveal a skill no one knew they had? Don't we want our intimate other to be someone who can be both a sexy lover *and* a responsible parent, practical or intelligent in some ways and adorably dumb in others? Many of us desire partners, family and friends who can be in touch with their emotions *and* available for our own vulnerability. People can be both young at heart and appropriately mature. Being multiple can be enlivening, preventing boredom and resentment creeping in. Ultimately, it's simply useful.

In the Pixar films *Inside Out* and *Inside Out 2*, Riley's emotions are depicted as inner characters, each of whom is lovable and can be embraced – literally by each other and metaphorically by the audience, Riley's parents and Riley herself. I suggest that you too can enjoy your inner multiplicity by embracing it; your configuration of parts, their burdens and beliefs, their inner relationships are what makes you who you are. However, it is sometimes hard to enjoy our parts – their extreme behaviours, their challenging thoughts and emotions, even their very existence. That's particularly likely if you had a rough time in childhood (see **Appendix 2**, about

Adverse Childhood Experiences and protective factors). The good news is that Internal Family Systems is likely to have a positive impact on how your parts interact and how emotionally regulated your system can be. No matter how unlikely it may seem right now, the goals of IFS therapy are achievable, part by part and step by step (Schwartz and Sweezy, 2020):

- freeing parts from their extreme roles;
- restoring or creating trust in the Self, the inner leader;
- achieving more inner balance, harmony and wholeness;
- becoming more Self-led inside and in the external world.

Parts as people

Whether or not we manage to enjoy our multiplicity, it does seem to be how we are wired. An explanation that I find helpful comes from researcher Zev Schuman-Olivier, MD, in conversation with Helen E. Lees, who explains multiplicity in terms of the way the brain organizes itself.[2] The brain automatically links thoughts, feelings, behaviours and sensations into a neural network, he explains, and then adds a sense of self (lower case 's') to that network. Dr Schuman-Olivier calls this process 'selfing', the making of something into an 'I' or a 'me'. This process happens over and over and is generally adaptive, as it enables a person to respond in a contextually appropriate manner. The researcher points out that we might not even realize we switch from one 'self' to another 'self' – in IFS language, from one 'part' to another 'part'. That's where IFS and other therapies with a mindfulness aspect to them come into their own: slowing us down, inviting us inside to notice the difference between different parts of ourselves and their contexts.

If our brain automatically 'peoples' itself, then no wonder the *Inside Out* movies featuring Riley and her emotions have been so popular. Like IFS, the movies refrain from demonizing

Riley's uncomfortable emotions, and although each character is named according to a single emotion (Joy, Sadness and so on) they are shown as far more rounded than that. The Pixar writers and IFS both know and show that it's easier, more effective, even more accurate to relate to any inhabitant of our inner world personally, as a person.

I am suggesting that you and I relate to our inner experiences as people inside of us. My inner people and your inner people, the sub-personalities that IFS calls parts, may even have similar roles, thoughts, emotions, roles and names or labels. Nonetheless, we will all still experience or sense our own inner world uniquely. My primary sensory modality is visual, so I see parts inside; but many people, including Dick Schwartz, do not. Treating parts as people, or personifying them if we perceive them as, for example, animals, shapes or colours includes imagining that they have:

- bodies (or shapes) of their own, sometimes with related characteristics like age or gender;
- names they choose, as well as those they may be given by other parts;
- inner relationships, loyalties and conflicts;
- thoughts of their own;
- beliefs from family and society;
- hopes, fears and intentions;
- roles they would prefer if they had the freedom to rest or change.

We need parts to function

Earlier I highlighted that, because of how our culture trains us to understand people, we look at ourselves and each other and can't 'see' our multiplicity. To get around that cultural bias, here's a slightly curious suggestion: I like to imagine that our parts move through the world in a similar way to how invisible people or creatures are depicted in TV shows and films. You know, footprints magically appear, things are knocked over, food goes missing, and so on. An invisible being makes itself known by its impact on and in the world.

If you replay an hour, a day or any random amount of time in your life as if you are watching a film (or listening to an audiobook, or energetically reminding yourself), you might very well spot various parts of you actively involved in running or moving throughout your life moment-to-moment. It's not necessarily as straightforward as having 'a mothering part' because you are a mother or stepmother, though it can be. Rather, let the traces of your inner people offer landing places for your curiosity to alight like a butterfly: Who is it that always knew she wanted to have lots of kids? Who is it that is fearful about the state of the world the grandchildren will grow up in? Who recalls being a carefree party animal at university? I hope you see what I mean. I was unable to have children, and I have parts that make themselves known at times in response to that reality. Some hold sadness, feelings of isolation and loneliness, while others feel relief at perhaps using fewer of the planet's resources. Meanwhile, I notice with appreciation the bittersweet gratitude my writing and authoring parts experience as they acknowledge that childlessness frees space – without which this book would not have been written.

Parts need the body

As I've suggested, the mismatch between the singular-seeming body and the multiple inner minds can be a source of confusion. But it is easy to reconcile that apparent paradox by thinking of the body as the house where all your parts live. If you are reading this book, it is likely that your existing outer-world family, if you have one, lives in a home of some kind. Whether it is rented, mortgaged or owned outright, you are probably involved in its upkeep, keeping it clean, presentable and fit for purpose. In just the same way, your inner family also has a home within that home: your physical body.

- The body can be a resource for parts.
- Parts are often noticed in the body.
- Parts often vie for control of the body.
- Parts show up or communicate via body symptoms.
- Parts use or inhabit a body differently from each other.
- One's body is often a battleground or source of conflict between parts.
- When the body is sick or suffering, parts understandably react.
- A part has its own body (or at least a shape or kinaesthetic sense).

Here's an example of the first and last point above. When I was working with a client I'll call Jacinta in IFS therapy, Jacinta's Self was interacting with a young part carrying a lot of distress. Spontaneously, Jacinta started holding and hugging her own body with her arms. I responded, 'Can she feel that, Jacinta? That big comforting, holding hug?' 'Yes, now she's copying me, and she can feel it; we're doing it together.' That brought tears of connection and relief.

Parts energize parts

Parts of people also 'energize' or 'attract' parts of others, in that we often enjoy being with and seeking out friends or colleagues with parts like ours (some people use the term 'energy' or 'vibe' instead of 'part'). That way, we can more fully embrace a part with a political stance or religious faith perspective and practice, or a part who enjoys going clubbing, and so on. This can work in a pro-social way – think joining a local choir, supporting a football team – or in more risky ways, like being swept along by others' extreme parts who flirt on the edges of criminality by doing drugs or shoplifting.

Another way that parts of one person can bring parts in another to life is alluded to in the old saying 'opposites attract': one part's extreme views or beliefs rile up someone else's part holding the opposite. In IFS systems thinking, we understand that **polarized** parts inside and between people are striving for balance and have positive intentions. When parts have a strong agenda, parts can align (like fans of the same football team) and polarize (like opposing political party members) in the outside world. Noticing our reactions to another or others can provide insights and information about parts inside of us.

Polarization

Parts (or groups of parts) in conflict often show up as protectors using different and opposing strategies to bring balance inside. These conflictual ways of being often take up a lot of energy and attention, block access to Self, and distract from approaching and healing exiles.

This, after all, is one of the reasons people go to therapy, to uncover what or who might be out of awareness and understand themselves more. The therapist holds up some sort of mirror to the client so that they can see themselves more clearly. The therapist noting their own parts' reactions can inform this whole endeavour. That's what therapy is for: self-knowledge, self-acceptance and self-healing, for which IFS is ideal.

Parts, like children, long to be noticed (safely)

The parts who show up as you go through this book may be young – inner children. This may come as a shock, and I want to point it out early.

As a psychotherapist for whom IFS was a postgraduate qualification, and as a long-term client suffering with developmental trauma and blessed with bookworm parts, I have learned about optimal ways of being with young children – and with young parts. These include:

- providing a 'holding' and 'containing' environment, with good enough safety, support and challenge;
- offering a permissive yet boundaried relationship (so the child knows who the adult or caregiver is, and that they aren't it);
- being actively interested in and curious towards young ones;
- waiting for the little one to unfold (not in a passive but in a witnessing way) at their own pace and to their own tune;
- delighting in and appreciating the child or young person (in a comfortable way).

Many of us do not receive these relational conditions in the outside world and spend time, energy and financial resources seeking them in therapy – or, less consciously, in our adult relationships with others. I strongly suggest that your young parts need care and nurturing from *you*, as mine do from me. Thankfully, Internal Family Systems has developed tried and tested practices to help us notice and relate to our youngest parts (more on that later).

Not that it's necessarily all going to be plain sailing. You may come to know parts who feel angry at being unnoticed, perhaps for decades; others may resist being noticed, as they have a position of power on the inside they fear letting slip through their fingers. Being seen and noticed can feel dangerous to parts who have been traumatized, neglected or co-opted into a parental war. Tread carefully, and Section 4, Troubleshooting, is there to help you when you encounter challenges.

Parts are contextual

Like humans, parts are contextual beings. Different parts come to the fore at different times, in different circumstances and in specific relationships, and to perform different tasks. When I was first learning counselling 20 or so years ago, we joked about one of the social habits in the UK which still endures. It's the 'script' to follow when meeting someone in the street, or more recently online: 'Hi, how are you?' 'I'm fine, how are you?' The joke in the training was that 'fine' stands for 'fucked-up, insecure, neurotic and emotional'. None of which is perhaps suitable to share in a passing 'nod' with an acquaintance or with a colleague on a work call! In my middle-class, privileged, pre-dominantly white part of the world, one's well-behaved, socially presentable and polite parts are front and centre when out and about. In that way, no one can tell other parts feel F.I.N.E!

In the UK, where I live, and in many white-dominated societies, Black men and boys are socialized into presenting certain parts that appear unthreatening, well-behaved, law-abiding. This is literally to survive the threats they often encounter, which include over-reactive parts of people in police uniforms (with or without guns, depending on the location). Black women are often dominated by a strong 'keep on keeping on' part, also for survival. In this country, brown-skinned women may feel perpetually stressed trying to please inner perfectionists from a long line of perfectionists on the female side.

Parts tend to get the opposite of what they intend

On the inside things have their own ways of working, just as in everyday life. As you observe your inner world, you will notice certain predictable patterns at play, some so predictable that some IFS practitioners call them 'The Laws of Inner Physics'

13

(Schwartz and Sweezy, 2020). One of the laws of inner physics is that the parts who are trying to protect us tend to get the opposite of what they intend, through no fault of their own, but as a function of their perceived role and task. In a tragic paradox, a protector will almost draw to itself the opposite of what it is hoping for.

The nearest metaphor or idiom that I can think of to explain this is the saying coined by Robert ('Rabbie') Burns, the Ploughman Poet, in the eighteenth century. In ploughing his field, he unwittingly turned up a mouse's nest. He wrote these lines about it in Scots, translated into English as:

> The best-laid schemes of mice and men
>   Go often awry,
> And leave us naught but grief and pain,
>   For promised joy!

The plans of the mouse (house-building if you like) and the plans of the ploughman (ploughing his field) were both disrupted through no fault of their own. Both were doing what made sense to them at the time, with the knowledge at their disposal. Neither deserves blame for what happened.

Taking it into more psychological realms, an inner critic's intention for their system may be vastly and diametrically opposed to the outcome it brings about. My inner critic, for example, was engaged for decades in what it experienced as a life-or-death struggle to keep me small and silent. My survival, or so it thought, depended on knowing I was *All wrong, all wrong* and acting accordingly. That way, it thought it could protect me from wrath and danger from without. But that effort led my nervous system to be in a constant state of hyperarousal, whereby the slightest criticism from someone close to me could feel like a full-scale attack. My inner critic's effort to protect me from the external danger led me to feel constantly endangered – the exact opposite of its intention!

You may have a similar inner judge or critical parent part like mine, with the best of intentions, who tries its best to protect you from external others with a constant barrage of *No, don't* or *Do it again, better,* or whatever it happens to be. However, their **agenda** of improvement may evoke a rebellious child part, who will reliably sabotage its best intentions by acting in ways that provoke the disapproval of others.

Parts who are polarized like that need help on the inside from Self, who can come alongside them, so they feel less alone and 'urgent' about themselves, their roles and their agendas. That inner Self can gently bring aid through offering a different perspective, and with gentle, compassionate curiosity ask: 'Are your efforts working?' Almost always, when a client's part is asked this in therapy, the answer is 'No'. The next question the inner Self can ask is, 'Are you interested in trying something different?'

Having an agenda

Protector parts hold agendas. Managers aim to control other parts (in their own system and in the outside world). Firefighters aim to restore inner equilibrium by any means necessary. Self, on the other hand, holds lightly and without attachment the intention of bringing balance, harmony and connectedness, as well as healing to parts and systems.

Journal prompts

Scanning for parts from activity in the external world

See if you can take a moment now to scan through a chunk of your week, day or hour to notice what parts of yourself might have been active. Alternatively, see if you can somehow notice or observe yourself in the moment as you go about your day. Maybe sometimes when you hear an inner thought or notice an inner urge to act, you could become curious: 'Hello, who said that?' 'Hey, who wants that? I'm curious to know more.'

Recognizing parts from a list

Below is a list (arranged in alphabetical order) to assist your curiosity about your parts. It lists possible names or labels for parts some of which are determined by the part's activity. See if you recognize any of your parts in the list. If you don't, that's okay too. This is early in your journey with me and this book. Also, you may not relate to those labels: you might sense parts inside in terms of colours, animals, cartoons or fictional characters.

Go ahead and make your own list, collage or drawing; take photos to represent parts, if you like. I've included illustrations of a couple of parts I'm familiar with: bookworm and inner child. And, if you do any of what I'm suggesting, get curious about who is doing the drawing or the listing or ...

What do you notice about your list, collage or picture board? Is someone inside judging some parts as 'negative' and others as 'positive'? Do you sense one part is coming up with the labels, or are parts offering their own self-identifying shorthand tags? Can you be curious towards that?

Remember, this is not like schoolwork – you do not need to learn this list, nor recall all that you have read so far. There will be no tests.

Figure 1.1   Bookworm

Figure 1.2   Inner child

A* student
Activist
Addict
Analyser
Angry
Anxious
Avoider
Blamer
Bookworm
Boss, the
Busy bee
Caregiver
Critic, the
Daydreamer
Distancing/dissociation
Dutiful daughter/son/child
Fearful
Fogginess
Hard worker
Hoarder
Independent
Inner child
Judge, the
Needy
News fiend

Numbing
Nurturing
Obsessive
Overwhelmed
People pleaser
Perfectionist
Persecutor
Procrastinator
Rage
Rebel
Recycler
Rescuer
Responsible
Saver
Shame-filled
Shamer
Shy
Soother
Spender
Sporty
Victim
Wanting to die
Working it out
Zoning out

2

Parts according to IFS (and more)

Have you ever had the experience of feeling hurt by or hurting a partner, spouse or someone close to you? I imagine you have. Consider for a moment how you reacted. Perhaps you burst into tears; maybe you shouted, slammed the door as you exited, or blocked them on your mobile. Sometimes when we feel let down and uncared-for, we can close or harden our hearts, clamp our jaws and carry on as normal.

Our feelings, behaviours, thoughts, dispositions and choices often change almost instantaneously and mostly outside of our conscious choice. Those changes are often subtle. But other times – especially when we're feeling hurt, or even hurting another – it's as though we become someone else, someone we perhaps would rather not have around. Now you know that 'other person' we become is what IFS calls a part. Other people have parts too; at times you will have noticed different 'versions' of those closest to you. People we know less well or in only one context or relationship may seem consistently themselves; nonetheless, IFS suggests that these people also have more than one part to them.

Three categories of parts

Now that we've explored the general principles of IFS, let's talk about how parts tend to interact within the inner system. As you go, it will help to think about the parts of people you know well – your own and those you might perceive in your loved ones, friends, colleagues and so forth.

My parts often use food metaphors to explain IFS concepts and processes, so I like to think of the different kinds of parts in terms of my favourite produce. There are different broad categories of vegetables, two of which are 'legumes' and 'crucifers'. Within these subdivisions are individually named vegetables: green beans and runner beans are different sorts of legumes, while crucifers feature broccoli (my favourite!) and cauliflower. IFS uses a top-level label 'parts' for all our individual subpersonalities. This overall category is then subdivided into two groups: the 'protectors' and the 'protected'. The protectors are further divided into 'managers' and 'firefighters'. The protected are called 'exiles' (see Figure 2.1).

Unlike vegetables, which merely lie alongside each other on the plate or complement each other in a smoothie or soup, parts are dynamic, relating to each other in certain common patterns. As Schwartz and Sweezy explain, our parts are distinct individuals, 'each with their own idiosyncratic range of emotion, style of expression, abilities, desires, and views of the world' (2020, p. 30–31). Together, all of a person's parts function as **a system**, like the members of one family.

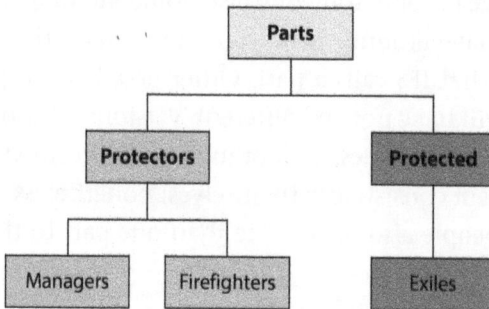

Figure 2.1 Categories of parts

A system

'The definition of a system is 'any entity whose parts relate to one another in a pattern ... [A system] is more than the sum of its parts ... In psychotherapy it works well to conceptualize and relate to individuals as *psychic systems*.' (Schwartz and Sweezy, 2020, pp. 25–8)

The IFS inverted triangle

First devised by IFS solo lead trainer Cece Sykes (2017), Figure 2.2 shows a variation on a common IFS diagram. Here you see an inverted triangle with a wavy horizontal line across it nearer the top – the downward-facing point – than the bottom. Imagine it as an impossibly top-heavy iceberg, with its tip concealed beneath the water. Above the line are the 'surface' parts, the outward-facing parts who protect us as we face the world. The two points of the triangle or iceberg above the water are labelled 'Managers' on one corner and 'Firefighters' on the other. The point beneath the waterline is labelled 'Exiles'. These parts are pushed under the water by the protectors up on top.

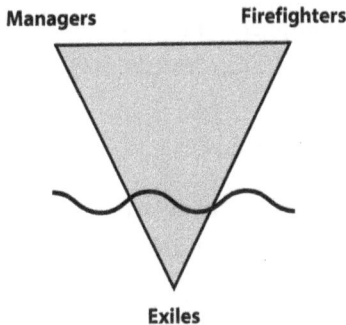

Figure 2.2 The IFS inverted triangle

When a part of us is hurt emotionally when we're very young, and that hurt isn't welcomed or is even shamed by the adults around us, the part gets pushed under the surface for the good of the whole system. The exiled part who holds that hurt – and the quality for which it experienced some form of rejection (e.g. intelligence, sensitivity, anger, sadness, creativity) – gets pushed down to stop it flooding the system with the hurt it is holding and from showing the rejected quality. Down below the surface of our awareness, in the cold and dark, the young exiled part can't grow and develop; it gets stuck at its young age, but at least it isn't as vulnerable to being hurt again in the future.[1]

As young people and adults, we go about daily life with young parts kept down this way, burdened by distress and painful memories and unlived life. These young parts don't escape because they can't; they depend on the rest of the parts, the way a little child depends on her family to provide for her. So, they're stuck, and they must make the best of it. Parts are designed to survive, and they learn to adapt to the people and things around them. Protectors not holding or carrying the hurt step up to keep the hurting ones below the surface; the managers work hard on a day-by-day basis to prevent the exiles escaping, and the firefighters are like emergency responders and jump into action if the managers can't cope and the exiles manage to push their heads up into our awareness.

Protectors: managers

As the name suggests, our manager parts tend to run our day-to-day lives in the outside and inside world. They do so in a proactive manner, with a future focus, anticipating what might result in exiles' emotional pain and forward planning to reduce that likelihood.

In modern Western societies, our managers often behave in ways like these:

- Approval-seeking, likable
- Caretaking of others
- Keeping things steady and stable
- Perfectionistic, critical, judgemental
- Rational, analytical and 'heady'
- Responsible, dutiful
- Success- and improvement-oriented
- Task-oriented, striving.

Though their methods can sometimes be quite harmful, our managers are also indispensable in our healing. It is often a manager part who takes us into therapy and chooses our self-help books. (You might take a moment to wonder which part of you decided to read this one.)

Since families and society tend to favour managerial behaviours, it is easier for many of us to identify with our managers and let them drive our **inner psychic bus** for long periods of time. Here's a personal example to explain. As an infant and child, I was often intensely frightened without having anyone available to recognize or meet me in my fear, which added to my terror and emotional distress. 'Heady' protectors were among the team who figured out how to protect me from intense fear by blocking *all* feelings with rational thinking. It wasn't until my early thirties that I came to realize that 'living in my head' and not feeling was no longer serving me – even though showing up as my rational manager had led to considerable success for me in the outside world. I readily remember the strangeness and quiet elation the first time I experienced being more than *just* 'my rational part', so identified was I with that part for so much of my life.

Experiencing yourself as *more than* a particular part suggests that the part has de-centred itself, stepped back from the steering wheel (for however long) – in IFS language, 'unblended'.

Inner psychic bus

A metaphor for inner multiplicity in which we can think of our parts and Self as journeying through life in a people carrier. Parts vie for control of the steering wheel, the route, the speed and so forth. Guiding parts into trusting relationships with Self and with each other gives Self more consistent access to the driving seat. And, yes, most of the parts onboard will be children, who really should not be driving a bus!

It's good to have managers inside, right?

As I mentioned in the last chapter, you can often 'see' or 'detect' parts through how you function and what you do in life. But you may be surprised to know that even those parts who manage our grown-up lives became stuck in their roles quite young, when the need to protect us first arose in our lives. When we turn inside and see how our managers show up, they will often appear as children or teenagers (invariably younger than our current age) – sometimes with a clipboard in hand or a string of pearls round their neck, but nonetheless shockingly young for the responsibilities they feel they must hold.

So, yes, our manager parts do important jobs inside us and outside in the world, and they also feel they must do them as *no one else will*. If they don't do what they do, *something terrible might happen*. Usually, alas, the dreaded 'something terrible' has already happened – at the exact moment in the past when exiles, the wounded ones, became frozen in time and the managers mobilized around them to ensure our continued survival.

Remember, our parts are doing the best they can with the hands they have been dealt. Like every part of every person, managers have **positive intentions** for the system they are part of. When the Self arrives to relieve them of their extreme roles, they bring immeasurable gifts to the system. I'm thinking of some of my inner writing team now, whose managerial gifts have made this book possible. The part of me who used to overfocus on others' needs and preferences now helps me monitor my own deadlines and keep going. A part who was committed to academic success now simply delights in producing books for other bookworms to read. And a formerly harried striving manager calmly and diligently helps me structure this book in a way that makes sense and takes feedback thoughtfully into account.

Positive intention of parts

Even though their extreme behaviour may not always result in beneficial outcomes, managers and firefighters are actively working inside the system with positive intent. When we notice a part is driving our inner psychic bus, we can appreciate them and be curious: 'How are you trying to help?' 'What is your positive intention for this system?' 'What are you afraid would happen if you weren't at the wheel?'

Protectors: firefighters

Let's turn our attention now to the second category of protectors, the firefighters. We often recognize them only after they have done their work, when we might say:

- 'That wasn't me, not the *real* me.'
- 'I always end up doing that when I'm with those two!'

When other people have spotted firefighter activity in us, they might say:

- 'That was so out of character – she's not usually that loud!'
- 'It was like someone else took over; he's normally careful about how much he drinks.'

We can also recognize firefighters in the moment if we really listen inside to our inner commentary, particularly the sorts of things we tell ourselves about behaviours we don't fully approve of:

- *It's no big deal, I just need that glass of wine at the end of the workday to ease me into the evening.*
- *It's the middle of the night, just one more episode, then I'll unplug.*

These last two everyday examples are typical of the sort of firefighters known as 'distractors' and 'soothers'. When we come home from work and begin to hear or experience hints of other parts inside screaming (or whimpering) for attention, these fire-fighters step in as emergency responders to prevent the exiles 'storming the gates' with overwhelming emotional demands. Firefighters are poised and ready to step in when managerial strategies fail – as they often do at the end of the day, when our managers might be exhausted after being hard at work for hours – with strategies of their own to soothe, calm or distract. The inner firefighter motto might be *Whatever it takes!* These brave and equally dedicated protectors are ready, as they perceive it, to save our lives – even if it means risking life and limb (or just potentially compromised liver functioning and lack of sleep).

Long before I first discovered Internal Family Systems, I became aware of my inner multiplicity after an actual real-life fire at my flats. My flat was on the top floor, and it was an outside-in fire ignited by sparks from an out-of-control bonfire nearby. After a long, harrowing and invalidating wait, during which the 999 operator told me several times that the building wasn't on fire, I was rescued by a real-life fireman and his real-life ladder. That latest in a long line of scary events over-whelmed the capacities of my heady and high-functioning managers to keep 30-plus years of emotional pain out of aware-ness. A food-restricting firefighter kicked into action, which helped to an extent, as did a part who specialized in avoidance and keeping up the pretence of normality. Nonetheless, the flames of my inner emotional pain burned bright enough to be detectable and began to break through inconveniently often. My overwhelmed managers could not keep the anguish of my exiles in check, so a higher-level firefighter stepped in, want-ing me to end it once and for all by suicide. Their method and means were clear. Somehow, I had the awareness inside that death was what only *part of me* wanted, and that there were other parts of me desperately wanting to stay alive, who had fought long and hard for that privilege. So, we sought help ... and now nearly 30 years later, here we are, writing to you.

Although that inner firefighter nearly killed me, its intention was purely good: it wanted only to protect me from being overwhelmed by the pain of my exiles, a fate it feared would be far worse than death. In dramatic ways and subtle ones, firefighters are always just trying their best to keep us from being overwhelmed. Their strategies include:

- Anger, rage outbursts
- Excessive anxiety, phobias
- Gambling, overspending, hoarding
- Preoccupation or obsession with an activity (excessive exercising, overworking, risky sexual behaviour)
- Self-harm (cutting, burning, etc.)
- Strategic eating (bingeing, purging, comfort eating, restricting)
- Substance use (alcohol, prescription and non-prescription drugs, etc.)
- Suicidal thinking or attempts.

This may seem like a rather frightening list, but firefighter activities can also be less alarming, and they often only surface at times of unusual stress or pressure. Do you recall I mentioned restricted eating earlier? That firefighter in my system started work in my early teens and went largely unnoticed. When the effect of its strategy was noted – by males – I would be praised for the improvement to my physique! This firefighter activity has since resurfaced a few times when my system has been under increased stress. Such firefighter activity often goes unnoticed both by external others and by ourselves, taken over as we are by the firefighter concerned.

When questioned, firefighters often feel trapped and desperate, but know of no other strategy or skill to employ to prevent overwhelm. If they are in an adversarial internal relationship with a particular manager or group of managers, as often happens, they may also fear losing status, control and access to the inner steering wheel. Like managers, firefighters are often very young. Though a firefighter may use an over-age activity to do its job, it's probably anything but grown up.

Unlike other therapy approaches, IFS does not view firefighter behaviour as pathological, but recognizes the protective intention behind it. IFS welcomes *all* parts, vilifying none. That doesn't mean to say IFS condones all behaviour, but the model insists that, within its context, a part's behaviour, thoughts, beliefs and reactions all make perfect sense. In IFS we negotiate with a firefighter to let the Self in the system help with the underlying problem of exiled feelings. We might also negotiate some sort of ceasefire or reduction in hostilities between a polarized firefighter and manager.

We can take this diplomatic approach because IFS recognizes the systemic nature of firefighter activity. It is never appropriate (though it would be understandable) to blame a firefighter for its behaviour, as if that protective part alone is the problem. A part who protects us with extreme behaviour can often be helped to take some responsibility for how it acts and potentially dial things down, but the problem it is trying to solve is system-wide. (More on this when we turn to exiles.)

If this all seems a bit bleak, don't lose hope yet! Stay with me; it may get a little worse before it gets better, but it will be worth it.

The protected: exiles

Exiles are the parts of us who hold the burdens of past **trauma**, undigested memories, hurtful failures in attunement from caregivers, and so on. To all intents and purposes, they are frozen in time in the past; they are repressed, ignored and denied access to the inner steering wheel. In a darker metaphor, they are imprisoned without trial and with no hopes of parole. Meanwhile, the protectors keep the exiles incarcerated, saying, *It's for your own good*, and *it's for the good of the system*. They truly believe it, too. There is truth and righteousness in this attitude, for it enables the survival of the system.

Facts of our biography give clues about how young our exiles might be:

- 'Dad died when I was eight.'
- 'I'm told my mother was in hospital for a long time after the birth of my baby brother when I was six.'
- 'Things turned really heavy when I made it to 16, so I ran away from home.'

In the dark ages of perinatal care in the 1960s, my newborn system survived being isolated and alone in an incubator for six weeks after a premature birth. I know now I survived that harrowing experience due largely to the valiant efforts of my protectors and exiles, some of whom I have not yet reached and connected with. These parts of me are very young, as exiles often are – remember, such parts have often remained the age they were when the bad thing happened.

Trauma

Our systems experience trauma when we perceive (consciously or subconsciously) a close encounter with our own death – whether because of a single high-impact experience, like a natural disaster or a violent crime, or an accumulation of numerous lower-level instances of deep suffering over time. Such experiences include being bullied or humiliated, which might cause a part of a person to wish they were dead. Also, any experience when one's mental or physical integrity (meaning one's sense of wholeness and completeness) was felt to be at stake, such as during and after a significant unrepaired rupture in relationships with caregivers.

Self is not a part

Beyond our parts is our ageless, whole Self, who cannot be hurt. Self is not a part. Richard Schwartz, the founder of IFS, considers the Self the most important contribution of the model to psychotherapy. In the 1980s, when he listened to his clients as they talked about their inner worlds in therapy, they told him that when their parts stepped back, there was a calm, compassionate awareness which they could feel at their core. When Schwartz asked them what part of them this loving presence was, his clients would often say simply, 'That's not a part, that's *me*. That's *myself*.' Schwartz heard that so often that he decided to call the phenomenon they were describing Self, spelled with a capital 'S'.

When his clients noticed this Self inside, it would invariably feel loving and connected towards all the parts in the system, the managers, firefighters and exiles. Over time, Schwartz and his colleagues and clients worked out how to bring Self and the parts together in ways that could free the exiles, relieve the protectors (with their consent) of their exhausting labours, and help them all let go of the burdens they bear.

Burdens

In IFS language, *burdens* are beliefs our parts hold that cause suffering. Our exiles carry our heaviest burdens, but our protectors often carry burdens of their own. Parts take these burdens on (particularly in childhood) when we are hurt, terrified, abandoned, neglected, shamed, invalidated, or met with extreme or repeated lack of attunement by caregivers. Even in families where parenting was generally 'good enough', due to differences in sensitivity or neurophysiology, parts can become burdened with feelings of worthlessness. Poignantly, some protector parts learn to perform their roles by taking on some of the rejecting qualities of the caregivers who (inadvertently or by design) gave a message of *you are not good enough, you are not welcome*, or *you don't belong*. They protect the rest of our system from the potential for rejection by taking on the burden of believing we deserve it.

The beliefs that burden our parts worked well enough in childhood to promote our overall safety. However, in adulthood, the roles burdened parts play in our systems tend not to serve us well. That is because they come from trauma at three different scales:

- **Personal burdens**, or 'identity burdens', arise from the part's own experience of life. For example, a part may believe *I don't deserve to be loved* because it didn't feel loved as a child in its family of origin.
- **Legacy burdens**, sometimes called 'relational burdens', are passed down to our parts from a parent or authority figure, based on the experience of that person or someone of a previous generation. For example, a daughter might 'inherit' from her mother the belief that *I don't have needs, I must tend to everyone else's*.
- **Cultural burdens** are those that enter a person's system from the social world they live in as they learn how to behave in socially acceptable ways. Richard Schwartz considers that the USA is particularly burdened by racism, patriarchy, individualism and materialism (Schwartz and Sweezy, 2020). Society in the UK is similarly burdened, as well as affected by its colonial past and by a culture of entitlement. When the burdened beliefs of our culture cause us harm, our parts often protect us by taking those beliefs for their own. Even without personal experiences or inherited beliefs, parts of people in the Western world often take on cultural burdens like *fat is bad, thin is good* or *boys don't cry*.

No matter where they come from, all burdens lead to imbalance; they constrain our parts by limiting their options and expectations of what's possible.

Among the most important axioms in IFS is the idea that *parts are not their burdens*. We don't let go of our burdened parts, we help them let go of their burdens. No matter how extreme the beliefs that burden them, all our parts are essential inner family members.

They need help returning to their original unburdened states of being. Unburdening our parts, ideally with the support of someone trained in IFS, is one of the most important things we can learn from the model, and I'll tell you much more about it later.

Parts thrive on appreciation and validation

Now that you know how your parts have been helping you in different ways, perhaps you can see them differently. How about you send round a word or two of appreciation inside, or give a psychological high-five to that multi-minded you in the mirror? (No pressure, it's just an invitation; parts can notice if they wish to or have the time and energy. In IFS, we always take no for an answer.) Appreciation for our protectors keeps our system running smoothly, like oil flowing through the engine of our inner psychic bus. Parts, like outer-world children, need to be loved, appreciated and helped to be children once more.

Another aspect of IFS that can be enormously helpful is validating our parts' experience. Think of a small child who is angry and making it clear that their sibling 'done them wrong'. It is not helpful to tell that small child to *grow up* or *get over it*. But it might help the child calm and be soothed if we acknowledge their distress, letting them know we understand how upset they are by what has happened and that their upset makes sense. Our parts also benefit from such validation. As with appreciation, validation comes from Self, the you-who-is-not-a-part.

To validate a part is to demonstrate that your Self supports the truth or value of what a part shares; it is to honour and recognize the part, its thoughts, feelings and behaviours as the truth of its experience. This is not the same as buying into the part's perspective – and certainly, parts don't have to agree with each other or with you. Each part has value and significance in the system as who and how they are. The protector who admits, *I have to shame her to keep her small, so no one can humiliate or reject her* – that part is as worthy of validation and recognition as the exile the protector shames. And, of course, the exile carrying the painful memories of being trampled upon and dismissed deserves acknowledgement and validation, too.

Blending and unblending

If your Self is always available to appreciate and validate your parts, to value them as they are and help them release their burdens, then why do your parts so often seem to be in charge? In IFS language, that is because they are often *blended* with the Self, who can learn to help them *unblend*.

The metaphor of the inner psychic bus and its passengers will help me explain these important IFS concepts. Imagine a bus of your choice full of emojis, each of which represents a person's face expressing a different emotion (grinning face, pensive face, thinking face and so on), or a different job such as 'woman student' or 'man farmer'. That is how we will represent our parts for the moment, as little emoji people in our psychic bus. Any one of these inner emoji people can come to the fore inside or 'blend' and start driving the bus. When that happens, from the bus's perspective, all the other emojis might as well not exist – there is just one person in the driving seat.

Steering the bus is what IFS calls 'blending'. When a part looking and feeling like the emoji that represents anger blends, we say *I am angry*; as on the bus, we naturally identify with the part who's driving, believing – in that moment – that *this is all of me*. It's as though the part feeling the anger has momentarily forgotten or put out of its awareness any exile it protects, as well as forgetting about Self's existence. It may or may not be aware of the existence of other parts. It momentarily dominates the inner psychic space.

Blending with a part isn't always a problem: sometimes it's a great help. Sometimes, a part with special skills or abilities *should* blend as fully as it is able when circumstances require. Here is a personal medical example. A few years back, I was having an invasive procedure as part of being prepared for surgery. I was conscious during the procedure, and many parts of my system really did *not* want to be. So, my parts decided by consensus to call upon a protector who is very good at helping us dissociate. This trusty part gamely took the wheel and supported the system by doing what it did best, and off we drifted.

Although it is completely normal and understandable for our parts to blend and 'drive the bus' of our consciousness, it can also be problematic and inconvenient, and lead to consequences we don't want. If a part of you is blending, then it will think, feel, act and present as you *on its own*. There's no inner multiplicity when a blended part is driving the bus – just a lonely child, driving a bus as though it were a grown-up.

The process of 'unblending', helping a blended part let go of the steering wheel of our inner consciousness so Self can lead the driving, is an important part of IFS practice and theory because emotional well-being comes from parts becoming aware of Self and trusting it enough to steer the bus. Later chapters will suggest ways to help parts unblend, as well as how you might respond to others when a part has taken over in their system.

Systems thinking

Remember that, like a bus with many passengers, each person is a system, a community. Before he founded IFS, Dick Schwartz was an expert in marriage and family therapy. He immersed himself in systems thinking when it became part of psychotherapy thinking and practice in the 1970s. Both these influences fed into the development of IFS. Systems thinking contributes some important concepts:

- IFS centres upon self-healing.
- IFS is a constraint-release model.

- Change is systemic rather than localized.
- Systems exist within systems.

One of the central tenets of IFS (though not unique to it) is the concept of self-healing (lowercase 's'). This is the concept and reality that a person (or any living system) has an inbuilt drive towards and wisdom about their own health and growth. Just as humans have physical self-healing mechanisms, so we have psychological self-healing mechanisms, both of which can be overwhelmed and need support at times. In addition, IFS teaches that the human system comes fully equipped to lead a harmonious life, internally and externally, but that things get in the way of this. What gets in the way is called in IFS a 'constraint', and these constraints block access to inner resources, wisdom and self-healing. The work of IFS, and working with IFS, is designed to highlight and release constraints, thereby freeing natural health and well-being, which includes the ability to self-heal emotionally.

Relationships between parts can also act as constraints – for example when two parts are polarized and there is an inner battle for power, or one part suppresses the other for a time only for the balance of suppression to shift and then shift again. Such inner conflict between parts takes up tremendous energy and focus; it creates stress and distraction preventing access to Self, the inner liberator, leader and healer.

A popular metaphor for the coexistence of Self and parts is that of the sun as a representation of Self. The parts are represented by clouds which pass in front of the sun and block it from our view and our awareness, but still the sun exists even if we cannot see or feel it. In this case, it's an apt metaphor, but don't let it set up in your mind an unnecessary binary of parts/ clouds = bad, Self/sun = good. Remember, all parts are welcome, we can't do without them, and they have positive intentions in how they seek to serve their system.

Another important aspect of systems thinking is that intervening in or changing one aspect of a system has an impact on other levels of the same system. For example, deeper work with exiles – often with trained support – is usually needed before an extreme protector will completely 'stand down' from its dedicated hard work. Similarly, intervening in one system has an impact on interconnected systems. A family system like yours or mine is made up of several interconnected systems, so it's important to bring Self-led patience and perspective to all interconnected systems in the wake of any individual change.

Why my husband and I eat lots of veg

Here's a real-life example from the system of my marriage, which interconnects my husband's internal family and mine. In the wake of multiple family deaths and various health issues in my late forties and early fifties, I sought out a Self-led nutritionist. Following functional medicine tests, I revised what I ate, adding various supplements to feed certain bacteria. After living in a family of origin fuelled by home-cooked food and where 'food is love', my system shifted to embrace the concept of 'food as medicine'. At the time, I alone made such dietary changes, including fermented food and drink alongside indulging in a cornucopia of vegetables and fewer carbohydrates. Now 15 to 20 years later, my husband makes our homemade kombucha and actively enjoys eating salad and vegetables. This, from a boyhood of eating only peas, shows an impact of a change in one system (mine) leading to behaviour change in another system (my husband's), without any agenda on my part! Interconnected systems are complex, so that result was hardly predictable. Rather than my husband's system embracing this change, it is also possible that his system could have polarized with mine and instead embraced highly processed foods!

Like systems in the natural world, human systems are embedded in other systems at every scale. An individual bacterium that helps ferment our kombucha is a tiny system, nested inside the microbial ecosystem of the fermented tea, which then becomes part of the larger microbial system of my belly when I drink it. Thinking this way, our individual systems are nested within our external families, communities and society overall, each of which can also be considered as a system of parts and Self. Within us, each of our parts has parts of its own – a heady thought we can safely leave to ponder another time. More important for now is the idea that all our parts also have Self. That means a part can, if it is willing and able, contribute its own Self-energy to the system.

A final point about how our parts work together in a system may sound somewhat contradictory. (My parts do enjoy a paradox, such as the idea that change occurs through deep self-acceptance, for example.) Parts are not equipped to lead, liberate or heal the inner system in the way that Self can, and *that's okay*. That is how it should be. This is similar to the way that children are not equipped to parent younger siblings or a parent or caregiver, and should not have to.

Having said that, adults who were parentified as children (had to look after others as if they were the parent rather than be parented themselves) make regular clients in this challenging modern world of ours and it does keep us therapists in work! It's a bittersweet pleasure to let parts in adult clients know that 'It really makes sense you feel a failure and not good enough because you took on a job as a child that you were not equipped for (through no fault of your own). You should never have had to parent others in that way.'

Why all this theory?

Primarily, I'm telling you all this because you have some interest in meeting your inner family, and understanding the basics of IFS theory will help you make sense of them when you do. Also, I'm the sort of person who likes to give people advance information about what to expect before venturing into the unknown. In addition, this theory will help you make sense of the case studies in later chapters. And the theory offers hope for what IFS has to offer:

- A non-pathologizing approach in which all parts can be welcomed and appreciated as valuable members of the inner family;
- Opportunities for protectors to feel less alone and more supported;
- Ways for exiles to get free from their captivity and return to the light of our awareness;
- The possibility of relief for parts through letting go of their burdens;
- Living life differently and with choice, not out of desperation and obligation.

There are many stories about finding long-lost family members, tracing previous generations and rediscovering our roots. These suggest and show that knowing who and where we come from is important. Being in connection with newly met siblings and relatives brings feelings of wholeness and completion. Finally getting to know the members of our inner family can bring an even deeper sense of internal well-being. You may never meet *all* your inner family members – remember, like the TARDIS, human beings are bigger on the inside. But coming to know as many parts of yourself as you can is valuable, life-enhancing and worthwhile.

IFS ideas to remember

- Parts are not problems to be solved.
- All parts, both protectors and exiles, have positive intentions for the system to which they belong.

- Strategies our parts used to protect us in the past may not serve us well in the present.
- IFS provides a new and transformative way to be with our parts.

Journal prompts

Starting to notice your parts

From the brief outline of parts so far, do you recognize any of your own inner family or team members as managers, firefighters or exiles? If so, list, draw or collage them; match them with their favourite music or lyrics, or even fictional characters. See if you can begin to sense that they are multi-dimensional inner beings. I say 'beings' because parts in some systems do not show up as humans but as animals, shapes, colours, cartoon characters or stick people. Sometimes, parts show up as bodily restrictions or sensations, not as images at all. Nonetheless, treat what shows up as if it's a person, and get curious.

Here are some questions to help you start:

- When you think a certain thought or have a certain feeling, do you notice a body sensation or movement? Maybe a frown appears, or your eyes become wide or tense.
- Are there times when you notice a change in your voice or the words you use?
- Do you sometimes feel or relate towards others differently, perhaps with unusual urgency or a change in energy?
- Does someone else notice a change in your behaviour and react to it?
- Do you notice a shift in how you feel, from one way to another? Maybe one part's shift is over and there's a handover to another.
- Do you feel a tussle inside? Different parts might be competing for the inner steering wheel.

If noticing parts is difficult at first, you might want to look at the section on troubleshooting.

Bringing curiosity to the beliefs that burden your parts

You may already have some sense of your own burdened or limiting core beliefs; you might have purchased this book in the hope it would help you be free of them and feel better about yourself. Without getting caught up in which type of burden is which, here are four suggestions about how you can become aware of personal, legacy and cultural burdened beliefs. You don't have to complete them all, of course. Please go gently: the idea is to find out new information about yourself and those in your world; it's not about blaming or shaming you or anyone else.

- Complete these phrases: 'I am ...', 'People are ...', 'The world is ...'. Here are some examples:

  - *I am useless, I can't get anything right.*
  - *People are just in it for themselves.*
  - *The world is a dog-eat-dog place.*

- Complete the following phrases and repeat them, trying different close family members of an older generation: 'My mother never ...', 'My father always ...', and so on. Examples might be:

  - *My father never expresses emotion.*
  - *My gran always praises my brother for stuff and ignores my achievements.*

- If something has happened that feels problematic, write it down. Then ask yourself, 'What does that mean about me?' or 'What does that say about me?' Like this:

  - Problem: *My boss never accepts any suggestion when it comes from a woman, but the same suggestion from a man is taken seriously.*
  - What that says about me: *My contributions don't matter.*

- Ask yourself if you have any 'shoulds', 'musts' or 'have tos' in any of the areas listed below. For example:

  - Education: *I must get all As* or *Girls have to try twice as hard at maths.*
  - Family: *My child should never suffer from mental illness* or *I must always be a perfect mother.*

Ability	Health (mental and physical)
Age	Job
Appearance	Language
Class	Location
Culture	Marital status
Education	Money
Ethnicity	Nationality
Family	Personality
Fertility	Politics
Gender expression	Race
Gender identity	Sexuality

As you go through the book, you will learn how to befriend the parts holding burdened beliefs. You may even be able to help parts release their burdens – though it's very important not to hurry towards that goal.

Remember, there are many ways people enter the sea, depending on personal preference and circumstances. With IFS, you can enter your inner world to varying degrees – only as deeply as feels safe and right to all parts concerned. If you've never been swimming before, you can safely paddle and get to know the parts of yourself you find near the beach. Working with deeply submerged exiles might be considered deep-sea diving, something that takes technique and training, and is safest done with another person. This will make more sense as you read, especially **Chapter 5**, which is about how IFS professionals help us heal our exiles. For now, simply investigating your parts and their beliefs, without trying to change them, will bring immense rewards on its own.

3

Learning about your Self

I am a non-identical twin, but my sister and I resembled each other enough that other people would often confuse us. As a young adult away at university, I regularly returned for weekend visits to where my family lived, accompanying my mother into town for mother–daughter time on Saturday and to church on Sunday. On such occasions, no one who approached me knew which twin I was, or they presumed wrongly, 'It's Cathryn, isn't it?' 'No, I'm the other one,' I'd say to end the conversation. Part of me would think resentfully, *Well, it wasn't me they were wanting to meet in the first place, was it?*

Being twins was hard for both of us, especially as our given identities were polarized. Abilities were divided between us almost without our input: 'She's the creative one; she's the academic one.' 'She's into horses; she's in a running group.' 'She's good with her hands; she reads.' As just one of 'the girls', I had no real sense of self and no idea of creating one; who I was felt dictated to me in words, deeds, through the ether, and via my genes.

University was a revelation and a liberation. After a false start when the death of my maternal grandfather had me quitting Cambridge, I embraced living in Leeds with everything I had available to me. A degree, a master's and a secretarial course later, I went into publishing as a secretary. During this time, I remained a dutiful daughter to my mother, an overly responsible hard worker, and an active churchgoer. I excelled at work and rose to a high level within the company before meeting and marrying my husband and starting a new life together on the other side of the country. By then I knew what I *did*, but not who I *was*.

The outside-in fire I told you about tipped me into a diagnosis of PTSD and eventually led me to therapy. That experience of therapy was where I first discovered the absence of a sense of self and the permission to begin finding myself. Fifteen years after beginning the journey inside, a year after my mother's death, IFS reached out to me and my parts reached back, and now here we are! Today, I not only have a sense of self, I have a *Self*. We all need both.

How do we define ourselves and identify?

Finding or defining oneself as an individual can be a full-time job. There are numerous ways to answer the question 'Who am I?' and if you are used to reading self-help books, you may already have many of your own answers. Maybe you've completed Myers–Briggs, know your Enneagram numbers, or can recognize your interactions according to the Parent–Adult–Child model of transactional analysis. Beyond psychology, there are many ways we define and find ourselves, perhaps through Tarot cards, angel decks or horoscopes. Perhaps we express our spirituality through being a member of a religion or other spiritual community: *I'm a lapsed Catholic; I'm a recovering alcoholic*. We may define ourselves as individuals by the groups we join, the teams we support, the relationships we have, or the jobs we do or can't do.

For good or ill, we may also derive our sense of self through our intersecting identities and social location in terms of power and privilege. Myira Khan's Identity Wheel diagram found in *Working within Diversity* (2023) helps therapists and clients become more aware of these social aspects of identity. Such reflective tools can help us locate and understand ourselves and to decide which aspects of our identities we might share that are not visible just from others looking at us. 'My name's Emma. I identify as a privileged, cisgender female, university educated, married, mostly able-bodied', I might say to introduce myself to those assembled on an IFS training or to attendees at a workshop I might be presenting.

However, such an introduction tells only part of the story of me (or of anyone). My social identity, like my Enneagram number or Myers–Briggs type, says little about who I am *inside*, about the parts of myself who don't show up in the mirror. And none of these ways of understanding myself captures the reality of my Self, the very core of who I am.

More about the you-who's-not-a-part

Self in the IFS sense is beyond identity. As we learned in the last chapter, the Self that resides within each of us is the calm, spacious energy that spontaneously emerges when our parts step aside from the seat of our consciousness. Your Self is the you-who's-not-a-part – in my case, the Emma-who's-not-a-part.

The qualities of Self

The IFS model has created some handy lists that help us notice the inner healing, liberating and leading energy of Self in ourselves and others. The 8 Cs are the qualities of Self as such; the Self's leadership will reveal itself through the 5 Ps. Beyond these commonly used lists of Self's characteristics, I like to use another

The 8 Cs	The 5 Ps	The AWOLs
Curiosity	Presence	Acceptance
Creativity	Playfulness	Availability
Courage	Perspective	Appreciation
Connectedness	Persistence	Welcome
Confidence	Patience	Open-heartedness
Compassion		Love
Clarity		
Calm		

one, which I cheekily call the AWOLs – qualities of presence that are the opposite of being 'absent without leave'. The AWOLs are attitudes of Self that are noticeably different from those of our hardworking, dedicated and burdened protectors. Together, these lists help us recognize Self as the essence of who we *are*, while our parts enable everything we *do*.

Connectedness

When parts of my therapy clients first learn about the concept of Self, they often wonder how to find their own. 'If everybody has a Self, where is it?' I tend to answer something like 'Self wants to connect, but it's up to you to give space for Self to be present. Self does not just barge through pushing you out of the way; it *connects*. When distressed parts want attention, we ask them not to overwhelm Self so a loving connection is possible. How does that sound?'

Self brings liberation

As someone who began life prematurely and spent time in an incubator, I'm not surprised that for much of my life I had a perpetual and uneasy sense of waiting (for something or someone unknown) and of feeling trapped (without reason). It is no wonder then that I found my way to becoming a perpetual therapy client, and a therapist, helping myself and others to be with their experience in ways that enable the body and mind to release and be free of what is painful and distorting and increases protection and rigidity. Experiencing a sense of inner freedom, having a generous amount of emotional and psychological freedom of expression, is something my internal family holds dear for my system and everyone else's.

As a client, I have sought and achieved elements of freedom through various creative expressive therapies; neurofeedback, which harnesses the brain's neuroplasticity directly; EMDR (eye movement desensitization and reprocessing); and finally IFS. Hopefully, many readers will also have experienced increased freedom in some way or another and of some duration through having therapy. In my experience and my clients', there is no more powerful force for freedom than Self, and IFS shows us how to make the most of its liberating potential.

The way Self liberates is beautifully expressed in this passage from Julia Sullivan, Suzan McVicker, Gregg Paisley and Pete Patton in 'Embodying IFS with Native American Clients':

> At times I get a glimpse, a taste, of a sense of miracle. When Self begins to connect to parts, and those parts begin to trust my Self, wisdom emerges like a gradual awakening from a long, long sleep ...
>
> This is why we wait. We go slow to go fast ... It takes time to behold the inner system, to learn and listen to it ... The pacing comes from within me, not my IFS helper ... Doing it 'to me' pains me ... My Self has always been free and powerful, naturally expressing 'power with' my parts. My Self supports my parts in not giving their sovereignty to anyone. Even those people I have started to trust. Those I trust don't want to conquer my sovereignty. They cheer me on when my Self liberates my parts. (Sullivan et al., 2023, p. 208)

IFS brings protocols and steps to follow which are best used when we have Self in the lead, free to drive our inner psychic buses while respecting the sovereign dignity of every part of ourselves. That is why IFS teaches practitioners to test for the presence of Self-energy. In the journal prompts I will be sharing ways for you to access and determine the presence or absence of your Self-energy, and take action accordingly.

Self offers leadership

As a family therapist and systems thinker in the 1980s, when he heard his clients talking from and about different voices or subpersonalities living inside, Schwartz readily thought in terms of an internal family. You can think of IFS as bringing family therapy inside yourself – and our internal families often reproduce the dynamics of the external families in which we grew up. If you picked up this book out of need, feeling a lack of leadership within you, then it is likely that the leadership of good-enough caregivers was lacking or only present intermittently in your family of origin.

This is not about parent-bashing and blaming; most parents really do their best. However, hormones and instinct can only get you so far in creating and raising a balanced and harmonious family! To be a good-enough parent takes conscious effort, reflection and choosing, over and over again. It's no wonder so many copies have been sold of the *Sunday Times* bestseller *The Book You Wish Your Parents Had Read (And Your Children Will be Glad That You Did)* by Philippa Perry (2020), offering the hope of becoming the parent you would like to be. The good news is that, while we can't change the way our parents led the families we grew up in, we can transform how we lead our inner families here and now.

Amazingly, when parts give space inside, this wise, caring, regulating inner resource IFS calls Self is already there, fully developed and ready to connect. Even if as children we did not experience consistently good enough caregiving, Self still has the wisdom, clarity and confidence needed to be the inner attachment figure our parts need to feel safe and loved.

How it feels when Self is leading

Self is a noticeable state of being in the body, which in and of itself brings healing. When Self is driving the psychic bus, our body can switch from fear-driven autonomic nervous system responses – our sympathetic nervous system's fight–flee–freeze survival responses and dorsal vagal collapse – to the spacious, easeful state of ventral vagal connection. The Self's leadership aids in regulating our hormones, our breathing, our circulation and so on.

Those physiological conditions create the conditions for inner harmony. When Self is leading:

- There is mutual respect among Self and every part.
- There is a distinction between roles: Self leads and heals, parts contribute according to their abilities.
- Young, unburdened parts can play and have fun.
- When conflict arises, parts turn to Self for mediation.
- There is a sense of continuity and inner wholeness.

Flexibility and fluidity characterize a Self-led system; Self can and does share leadership with parts when circumstances and tasks call for their expertise. Certain parts are best suited for certain contexts, and at times it can be fun, thrilling or sexy when certain parts take over. Some parts of us excel at the labours of grown-up life; others let us experience childlike joy. If the system is Self-led, then parts can come and go from the driving seat with relative ease and make way for Self when their work is done.

What Self is not

Before we move on, I want to offer some clarifications about what Self is *not:*

- **A concept you learn.** Self-energy needs to be experienced first-hand on the inside; it cannot be understood into existence. All this theory I am sharing is but groundwork for those parts who need or want knowledge upfront to risk experiencing something new, and potentially radical (i.e., meeting Self on the inside, noticing Self on the outside).
- **Invulnerable.** Your parts may initially equate Self with authority figures or leaders in the outside world, which may well give the wrong impression of Self's nature. 'Leader' in today's capitalist society is a loaded term, confused by the loudly proclaimed 'leadership' of social-media influencers, billionaires and tyrants. This is not the sort of 'leader'

I want you to think of when you think of Self. A Self-led person inevitably and paradoxically welcomes their own and others' **vulnerability**.

- **A saint.** Don't confuse Self-as-inner-leader with the modern world's spiritual figures or gurus, political exemplars or humanitarian heroes. Nope! Self is a spiritual being, not a particular kind of person – not Gandhi or Mother Teresa, but an instance of Atman, imago Dei or Buddha nature. Also, unlike politicians and other world leaders, who seem out of reach, living in another world, and uncaring about 'the little people', Self offers potential *daily* leadership, fully present in the ordinary course of human life.

- **A result of adulthood.** If becoming an adult meant we had easy access to Self, I would not be writing this book and IFS therapy would not be the global phenomenon it is. Age per se has nothing to do with accessing Self; children can and do access Self-energy, and adults frequently can't and don't.[1]

- **Constant enlightenment.** Some people familiar with IFS talk about being 'in Self' as a desirable state of being, something we could arrive at once and for all. I take a different view: rather than trying to be 'in Self' rather than 'in parts', IFS helps our Self establish harmonious and loving relationships *among* our parts. The inner family consists of all its members.

- **Nice.** Avoid succumbing to Western society's 'tyranny of nice'; Self is not some pleasant, possibly elderly and strangely invisible relative who dishes out metaphorical pats on the head and snacks to keep parts 'happy'. Self is a force not only of compassion, but also of courage, clarity, perspective and confidence.

Once parts unblend sufficiently, Self is available as an energetic or spiritual 'good-enough parent' on the inside and one that you might like to be on the outside (Vincentz and Bubbers, 2023).

Self

In IFS, the Self:

- brings healing and transformation;
- cannot be damaged or broken;
- does not attach to an agenda;
- welcomes every part, no matter what;
- has intentions for healing, connection and harmony;
- is a relational resource without fear;
- is fully developed and doesn't need to grow;
- can be overwhelmed or pushed out of the body by parts;
- is present when parts give space.

Self's leadership is non-hierarchical

Self offers liberation, leadership and healing – but this in no way implies an inner hierarchical leader with the one-up, one-down relationship that occurs among leaders and followers so often in the outside world. Self leads by nature and has no need to control or be 'top dog'.

That is why our parts can and do feel safe being vulnerable when Self is leading. A leader whose heart melts and opens to another's story (on the inside or the outside) is going to feel in that moment like a friend, a comforter. That sort of leader is someone to turn to as a resource, in the way that one turns to a loving canine or feline companion or goes to a favourite river, rock or tree to be 'held' and nurtured. There is no hierarchy needed or existing there, but mutual connectedness and presence.

Self has no needs and thus no expectations or demands of parts. It cannot feel threatened. Similarly, Self has all it requires and thus experiences no scarcity. This vanquishes any need for domination in order to take, hoard or capitalize on inner resources. Self is enough for all, doesn't need to be grown or developed, and cannot be reduced or damaged. From that place of infinite plenty, Self's nature is to connect, validate, respect and be.

The qualities of Self help our parts let go of any drive for an inner hierarchy. Before meeting and relating to Self, burdened parts are often in conflict, reaching for power and control. Self's non-hierarchical leadership frees the whole system from such exhausting power struggles. When Self has relationships with parts, there is the potential for protectors to quit extreme and demanding roles and do work they enjoy and can thrive doing instead. Exiles who have unburdened just relax into being themselves, at peace and at play. Parts who no longer have to perform for our survival can just *be*. And like all parts, all humans are equal in their beingness; in this way, IFS is inherently equalizing.[2]

Vulnerability (Redfern, 2023a)

Being Self-led means being appropriately vulnerable, which is to hold a workable, live perspective whereby you know, act from and are aware of your own simultaneous woundedness and healing, while also relating to others as being the same way: whole, wounded and protected, all at the same time. Vulnerable Self-leadership also contains an ability to not have to know, do and control, but to be, be with and welcome alternate or multiple realities. I have come to see the terms 'vulnerable' and 'vulnerability' as indicating emotional or psychological health.

How Self helps parts heal

As I have mentioned elsewhere, Self is a transformational relational resource. To be in the presence of Self, yours or another's (recognized by any of the C or P qualities and AWOLs) feels healing; healing enables still greater access to Self, and so the virtuous cycle turns. Richard Schwartz and others have identified certain steps that Self uses to help parts heal. We will go into this in more detail in Section 2 of this book, but I want to explain the process here to show *how* Self does what it does.

IFS talks about this process as 'the 6 Fs'. When you have a part of your system in mind to learn about (and it's probably wise to begin with approaching a protector), you'll generally proceed like this:

1 **Find** the part – as a mental image, a bodily sensation, or however else it appears.
2 **Focus** on the part with calm attention.
3 **Flesh out** the part – see or sense its presence as vividly as you can.
4 Ask, 'How do I **feel towards** the part?'

This simple question helps us recognize if Self is leading. If the answer to this question is compassionate, welcoming or curious – any of the C qualities or AWOLs – then you can be sure that it is your Self in the seat of consciousness, relating to the part you are focusing on. If the answer is anything else – *annoyed, afraid, impatient* and so on – you'll know another part of you is in charge. If that's the case, you'll ask that part to give Self space (momentarily, not permanently) to continue the relationship with the original part. And if it can't or won't, you'll simply turn Self's attention towards the part who intervened. Making sure Self is leading when you relate to your parts is important, because only Self is qualified to perform the last two steps of the process:

5 **Befriend** the part, offering it unconditional compassion and goodwill.
6 Address the part's **fears**. Protector parts who bear burdens do so because they feel they must in order to prevent a fearful outcome – being abandoned, losing face, dying and so on. So Self sets the table for healing by seriously considering the part's concerns – not dismissing them out of hand.

How did you feel inside when you read those steps? Some of your parts might have felt queasy about the idea of being focused on and discussing their fears, and rightly so. If they haven't come to know your Self well, they have no reason to trust it. Trust your parts' concerns; after all, they are trying to take care of you. If you encounter hesitation in your system at the thought of venturing inwards, I suggest having someone experienced in IFS with you, to whom you can turn if you find yourself out of your depth.

Self beyond the self

While the word 'Self' suggests individuality, the Self-energy we encounter within us is not an isolated entity but an instance of something far greater. IFS folk sometimes speak of Larger Self, or SELF, the more expansive and less individual nature of the Self in each of us.[3] Larger Self is transcendent by nature, a kind of infinite beingness beyond individuality. This field of being is the source of the personal Self in you and me, in the way that the imago Dei or Buddha nature are terms for that aspect of the supreme principle or ground of being in the universe contained within individual humans.

In their composite narrative, Indigenous IFS practitioners express the transcendent aspect of Self in a particularly eloquent way:

> The SELF is called many things. My favourite name is 'GUS' for Great Universal Spirit. The SELF, the Creator, is manifest in all of creation and is the connecting energy in all our relations. It is the SELF that my Self connects with in ways that are undefinable, indescribable. Like love, you know what it is if you've experienced it. (Sullivan et al., 2023, p. 207)

Lifesavers and role models

Just as we can learn to access the Self within us, we can also perceive the Self in others. Though I wasn't aware of it at the time, I had powerful experiences of others' Self energy in my own extended family. My father was largely absent due to work during our first 16 years, so my sister and I often lived with our mother and her parents, either in their home or in ours. This meant childcare on tap and my mother could continue working (important for financial reasons); for me, it meant I had access to my Grandpy. I didn't recognize it at the time but he's what some might call a lifesaver or a protective factor (see **Appendix 2**) and was the closest I got to a relationship with someone accessing Self-energy. Grandpy was playful – he taught me card tricks and did magic tricks. He had perspective – he seemed to see and welcome more of me than anyone else, no matter what. (When I got angry, he'd say in a playful way, 'She's rattigan.') He was full of what I now call AWOLs – I experienced him as accepting, welcoming, open-hearted and loving.

His loving presence was all the more remarkable considering his life. He was born the youngest of ten children in the 1890s, survived the trenches of World War I, and had a troubled daily relationship with a traumatized wife long before trauma was 'a thing'. Yet, somehow I was able to love and be loved by Grandpy, one Self to another. His long, slow home death and dying was deeply impactful on my system in myriad ways.

You, too, will have experienced someone or something – a caregiver, a four-legged friend, a place in nature – that embodied Self-energy for you, or gave you access to Self in their love, attention, acceptance, curiosity and more. Maybe you have embodied those qualities for someone else. See if you can be curious and let these relationships and those occasions come to mind over the course of reading this book. They might resurface in a bittersweet way, so be gentle inside if you can.

Noticing Self and parts in the body

In the last chapter, you explored ways of noticing your parts in action. As you get curious about your own embodied Self-energy, you'll start noticing how it feels when Self, rather than a part, is driving your inner psychic bus.

A reminder: the noticeable presence of parts is okay. We all have parts; we couldn't live without them. And in IFS, all parts are welcome – exactly as they are. Some of our parts might not want to be noticed. Others might appreciate an opportunity to be met and 'got' by Self on the inside. As you bring curiosity to your inner world, be as slow and gentle as is necessary for the most sensitive of your parts, those who are reluctant to open to anything new, or even 'allergic' to change or perceived expectations. The following prompts need not be a bother nor a disturbance to your parts, merely an exercise in curiosity and awareness. Because everyone's nervous system is different, feel free to adapt them to your own neurology and ways of being.[4]

Body tension and patterns

- How soft and mobile are your jaw, shoulders or forehead? Many of our protectors brace us in these areas, which can be detected in stiffness or holding.
- How are you holding your head? Many of us have a head tilt of one kind or another that can provide an interesting signpost to finding an active protector.
- What about your feet? Do you feel grounded, and how can you tell? If seated, are you balanced over both sitting bones? Some of us sit with one leg crossed over another, which a part gives a 'jiggle' to it.
- What about your posture? Is there a soft stability and fluidity? Some of our parts tend towards a collapsed slump or tight uprightness.
- How relaxed or soft are your eyes and your gaze? Many of us notice parts when we feel how wide and staring are our eyes, how piercing our gaze. Other parts might be active if our eyes are unfocused, inward or sleepy.
- What about your breathing? Is it smooth and deep or shallow and quick? When a part of us is helping us concentrate, many of us notice we hold our breath, almost as if we 'forget ourselves' in the task at hand.

Voice and speech

- How do you experience your voice? Is it loud and insistent, soft and gentle, clipped and terse, rich and resonant? (Did you notice any vocal 'tells' for parts you became aware of from engaging with the last chapter?)
- What about your use of language? Is there judgement present or curiosity, attachment to an outcome or desire to control, or is your wording openly descriptive and accepting?
- When you talk about your experience, do you notice yourself speaking *for* parts of you, in so many words? For example, 'Part of me wants to go out tonight, another part really wants to stay in.' That's probably your Self, reflecting on your system. Or is a part using your voice to speak *from* itself? 'No, I'm not going, I'm too tired.'

Movements and energy consumption

- Do you notice repetitive, intense, restrained or incomplete movements? Sometimes after I've had a body treatment and can access more embodied Self-energy, I recognize moving in a more relaxed, freer way and my centre of gravity feels lower down in my body.
- Does doing things a certain way drain your energy, leave it the same, or increase it? Many IFS professionals find being in Self-energy with clients less draining than when they work using other modalities where parts might be more to the forefront.

Response from others

- If it feels okay enough, become curious about how others receive you and respond. Does their curiosity increase, and they become more open, or do they feel more closed to you, do they avoid or come back with an 'attack' or a 'fix' or to express hurt?

Noticing (or being told about) the activation of other people's parts can be a powerful way to distinguish between the activity of parts and Self in your system. Becoming aware of how my parts responded to my husband's helped me to see the part in me that initiated what could be called a 'vicious cycle' between us. When I was feeling rejected by someone, a hurt and confused part of me would say to my husband, 'I don't understand why they did X'. To which a helpful problem-solving part of him would reply, 'It's because you A and B and they X and Y.' But an explanation was not at all what my system needed in a moment of hurt – so another part of me would take over, verbally lashing out at my husband for 'mansplaining', or just erupting inside while exiting the room with feeling. My husband would be left bewildered and confused as his assistance was brushed rudely aside.

Over time and with curious introspection, I have come to realize that a whole lot happens beneath my surface before the part with confusion speaks up. Let's track the sequence of occurrences following the initial 'rejection':

- So fleetingly as to be barely noticeable, an exile in me feels upset and disappointment at another person's behaviour towards me, which it interprets as rejection.
- A protector detects the exile's hurt and wants to be angry at the 'rejecting other'. However, as in many people's systems, other protectors quickly rush in to prevent that part from protecting with anger, which they consider unacceptable and unsafe.
- Instead, in steps a protector to protect me from the exile's hurt in a subtle way: it uses tangly, twisty confusion to block the angry part, while shielding me from the disappointment of the exile. 'I don't understand why they did X', this part says.
- At this point a part of my husband, possibly a 'heady' intellectual protector, offers a rational explanation for *why* the other person did whatever it was that my exile perceived as rejection.

- Oh dear: that's not at all what my system needed to hear. My exile perceives my husband's explanation as yet more rejection – the needs of my parts for acknowledgement, validation and soothing are not being met from outside.
- But before the exile can express its pain, the part who uses anger steps in and lets rip at my husband or causes a 'huff' of an exit, distracting me from the emotions inside by blaming him outwardly.

It turned out that, in this repeated scenario, my husband was just the middleman. Nowadays, I'm more able to notice when an exile inside feels rejected, so my Self can offer it support and comfort. The part who uses anger to protect me from that pain isn't triggered; and the part who uses confusion to protect me from anger doesn't have to draw my husband into it by saying 'I just don't understand'. In fact, when I hear that part say *I don't understand* inside, that is my signal to see if there's a part underneath carrying hurt that my Self, the Emma-who's-not-a-part, can respond to if given the space to be present. That way, in time the part might feel heard and valued by me and might not even raise it with my husband. Or I might say, if it was important, 'A part of me felt hurt earlier, but they're okay now.'

Journal prompt

Looking out for Self-energy

When your Self is driving the inner psychic bus, you have access to the 8 Cs: clarity, calm, curiosity, confidence, creativity, courage, connectedness, compassion. When you can't access *any* of those qualities, a part of you is probably driving instead. Remember, that's okay! Parts are active all the time, and we need them to be. It's just that sometimes, we ask them to relax a bit so that more Self-energy is available inside, for them and for other parts.

I suggest you get curious about when and where you have accessed any of these C qualities. Often, this happens spontaneously and without effort, in the presence of natural beauty, human frailty, a loving other (four-legged or fewer) and so on. Similarly, you could be curious about when you have experienced, witnessed, seen or felt any of these qualities in another, whether towards you or towards someone else. There is plenty of space on the diagram (Figure 3.1: The 8 Cs) for you to jot notes or draw images as a reminder should you wish.

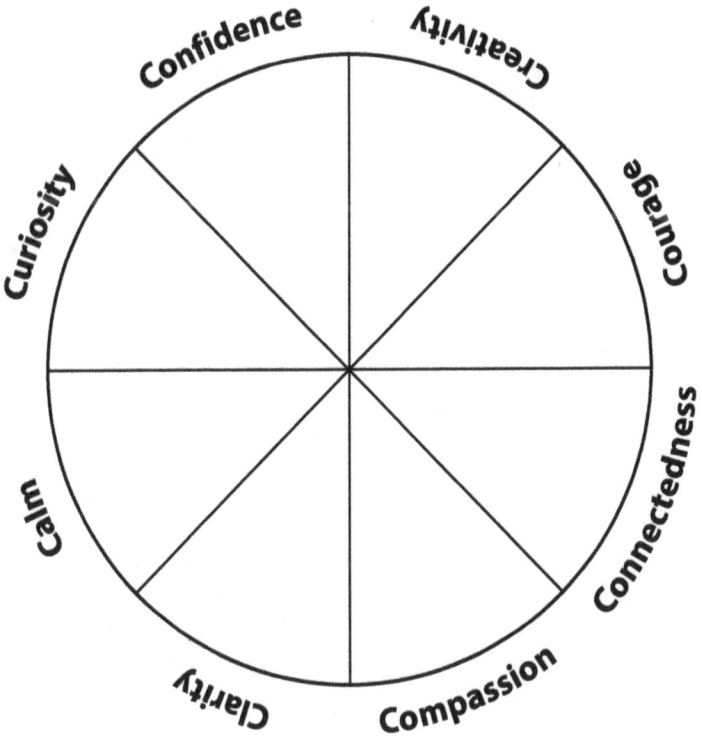

Figure 3.1 The 8 Cs

Section 2
KEY IFS PRACTICES

4

Befriending and updating our parts

In this section, I introduce key IFS practices across two chapters. **Chapter 4** focuses on you getting to know the members of your inner family and shows how Dick Schwartz led me in meeting some of my parts in a demonstration session to bring IFS theory to life. **Chapter 5** introduces IFS as a healing modality or method by showing how Dick helped me heal an exile of my own.

Who wants attention?

Generally, in IFS, and certainly at the beginning of using this powerful model, it's best to get curious one part at a time. It's possible that at first you might label everything you feel, sense or notice as belonging to different parts, which can get overwhelming. Alternatively, you might find you are drawn to lumping everything you notice inside into a single composite part. If you can, hold these tendencies lightly in mind as you enquire; the more you explore your inner world, the more clearly you'll come to perceive your parts as they are from their own perspective. You can ask and check things out with parts as needed. 'Just ask' is a mantra in the IFS community; rather than presuming in advance we know all about a part, we remain humble and tentative, treading with care to allow each part to reveal itself (or not).

The ideal time to meet a part is when there's plenty of time, few distractions, and a curiosity to let things emerge organically and gradually. I think of IFS, and curiosity especially, as 'emergent'; as we are curious, things emerge, and what emerges always transforms, changes and develops in some way. I have a very visual system, so think of this in terms of old-fashioned darkroom photography. I'm in a red-lit room swirling paper in fluid, and as I watch curiously, hopefully and with welcome, something gradually emerges on the paper to be seen and engaged with.

We get to meet our parts when they *want* to be known, not before. How do we recognize when a part of us wants attention? To explain, I want to show you how a part of me 'asked for attention'. In 2016, I attended an IFS Level 2 training in Sheffield, England, which took place over two blocks of five days. IFS Institute trainers – in this case, Richard Schwartz himself – do live demonstrations to show theory in action as a bridge to practice.[1] Naturally, many trainees put themselves forward for the opportunity of 'having a demo'. The method of choosing the 'client' was determined by each applicant choosing a card blind. I drew the highest card, the Ace of Hearts.

This was relatively early in the life of IFS UK, and I agreed to let the demonstration be videotaped so that senior members of the IFS UK team could use excerpts from it in future training courses. Instead of the American demonstration videos that were available at the time, this one would be 'homegrown' in the UK. That is how I come to have a precious transcript of what occurred to share with you now. (More recently, and very understandably, recordings of demos are generally not permitted.)

Dick asked if I had a part in mind to attend to, and I did. Having had my eyes well up with tears on and off throughout the training, I was curious about the part showing up in my tearfulness. That indicated where a You-turn was needed. As you'll remember, a You-turn is an act of turning away from the outer world and becoming curious towards our own internal experience. In IFS training, the part we want to meet is usually termed the 'target part', but you might prefer another term such as 'focus part', or like me you might identify the part by how it feels or shows up: my 'tearful part'.

The 6 Fs in Action

My session with Dick will show you just how IFS builds relationships between parts and Self. You'll see him using the '6 Fs' I've mentioned. The steps are usually listed in a specific order, but you might not follow them in that order every time, and you can always circle back and use each of them more than once. (As you'll see, Dick improvises with them, too.) Here they are again, in more detail:

1 **Find** the part you wish to befriend by placing attention or curiosity on it. Parts are often found in or around the body, though they sometimes emerge as thoughts or language instead.
2 **Focus** on the part by noticing how it shows up. If you see the part in your mind's eye, you might notice its age, clothing or appearance. If you experience it as a voice, you might notice how it sounds or the words it uses. If it's more embodied, you might notice how it uses your body, the energy it brings with it.
3 **Flesh out** the part by being curious about it as a person – even if it shows up in a non-human form – with its own beliefs, history, motivations, hopes, behaviours, relationships to other parts. In this way, you experience the part as separate from other parts and from your Self.
4 Ask yourself, 'How do I **feel towards** this part?' Accepting, welcoming, open-hearted? Curious, antagonistic, judgemental? If you feel anything other than one of the qualities of Self-energy, then you're blended with another part who is reacting to the one you've focused on. If that's the case, ask the part with the reaction to give space, with an assurance you will touch base with them later. Or have the reacting part become the **focus** instead of the one you started with.
5 Once you can access some Self-energy towards the focus part, be**friend** it by sharing your curiosity to learn more about it. If you are feeling compassion or any other C quality towards the part, share that quality with it. An important aspect of be**friending** is to check the 'hook-up' – we get curious about whether the part is receiving our curiosity (or compassion etc.). When be**friending**

67

parts, we notice their response to Self's presence: there may be a softening or a feeling of relief, or gentle tears may come, for example.

6 The sixth F is being curious about and addressing the protector's **fears**. We might ask the part about its fears of other parts or of change in general, and about what it is afraid would happen if it stopped doing what it feels it must do to keep the system safe. Speaking from your Self, you then address these fears in a systemic, sensitive way with clarity and connectedness. Addressing a part's fears can involve asking what the part needs from you to feel safer – perhaps a promise that you'll return and get to know them further, or reassurance that you won't let another part take over.

Finding and focusing on parts using trailheads and triggers

Becoming emotional (the tearful feeling) is an example of what IFS calls a 'trailhead' – a sign marking the start of a trail or track to somewhere. In UK English this term might be translated as a 'signpost'. The journalling prompts I've been providing at the end of each chapter have shown you how to pay attention to such signposts, which might be:

- a body sensation
- a change in breathing
- an emotional response
- an extreme or unexpected reaction
- an impulse or urge
- a memory
- a thought.

Parts often show up in my system as body sensations, which gradually become part-like in that emergent process I liken to a developing photograph.

Here is some dialogue from my demonstration session with Dick, with trailheads underscored. The boldface type shows where Dick is using the 6 Fs we discussed in the last chapter, which I'll explain in more detail later.

> DICK: Okay, so you'd like to get to know that <u>tearful</u> part? (Dick is ascertaining the presence of curiosity towards the target part to see if Self is present.)
> EMMA (nodding): Yes.
> DICK: As you think about going to it, is there any fear that comes?

In a public session like this, it is usual for some parts to be concerned. Protectors perform specific roles or jobs in the external world, but on the inside they work hard to block access to the potentially overwhelming feelings of exiles. In a public IFS demonstration, my protectors were rightly wary.

> EMMA: Yes.
> DICK: So, let's start there. **Focus** on the fear of going to the <u>tearful</u> part. See where you **find** this one in your body.
> EMMA: Mm (curling both hands inward and gently pushing them into my stomach). My <u>stomach is doing funny things</u> and my head (indicating with a hand the back of my head).
> DICK: Okay, so we'll start with your gut — it might be two different parts.

Dick was right, these were two parts, and we went first to one and then to the other until they agreed to let us meet the tearful one.

In IFS terms, we find trailheads when our parts are 'triggered'. I rather dislike the popular idea of being 'triggered', given its association with guns. I prefer the term 'activation' myself. But the idea of being 'triggered' is common enough among psychotherapists and on social media that it bears discussion. When we say we have been triggered, we mean that something we have experienced by any of our senses (or more than one) has aroused in us feelings, memories or echoes of an earlier distressing experience. For some of us loud noises are triggering in that they activate our sympathetic nervous system or fight-flight-freeze responses. The trailhead I brought into the session with

Dick was a part's tearfulness. That reaction had been triggered by something positive – namely, seeing or sensing loving Self-energy in action during the training. This triggered a part of me who felt unlovable.

Feeling towards a part and learning about its fears

Let's return to my session with Dick to watch the process play out. We've already had two of the Fs – 'find' and 'focus' – when Dick asked me to focus on the tearful part and see where I found it in my body. Then, when he asked if there were any parts who were concerned about getting to know the tearful one, the feelings in my stomach were a trailhead to a protector, and we turned to that one instead.

The steps of the 6 Fs sometimes flow into one another in the moment, and your Self will know when to let that happen – just as Dick did with me. 'Fleshing out' a part, the next step, can be done in many ways. In this case, Dick asks if it's okay for me to let the part associated with the stomach to blend more fully with me – to take up more room in my body and metaphorically sit in the driving seat of my inner psychic bus. Because Dick is confident in the presence of his own Self-energy and ability to 'befriend' any of my parts, he trusts that he can address my protective part's fears, which will help it relax and let us return once more to the tearful part I was curious about at the outset.

At this point, Dick asks the crucial question to ascertain whether my Self is present:

DICK: Just tell me how do you **feel toward** this one [the one associated with the gut]?
EMMA: I think I'm quite strongly blended with it. It's quite prominent.
DICK: Would you like me to speak to it?
EMMA: Yes.

DICK: OK. So, are you there?
GUT PART: Yes.

Recognizing these parts are driven by fear, Dick cuts straight to the chase and is curious about that. (He's effectively bypassed the 'befriend' F, which was fine as this part trusted him and wasn't the main focus of the session.)

DICK: So, you're afraid to let Emma go to the tearful part, is that right?
GUT PART: Yes.
DICK: Could you tell me a little about your **fear**?
GUT PART: Fear of disintegration.
DICK: That if she goes there, she'll disintegrate.
GUT PART (nodding): Yes.
DICK: OK. What would that look like if she were disintegrated?
GUT PART: An actual physical falling apart.
DICK: OK. Can you tell me a little more about why you think that might happen?

Dick continues to extend curiosity to the protector, specifically to learn more about its role in the system and in relation to the tearful part we've agreed to focus on when we can.

GUT PART: She's fragile. She's always been fragile.
DICK: Ah ha. So, you've kind of been holding her together for a long time?
GUT PART: (Considers this.) Yes, that makes sense.
DICK: That fits for you?
GUT PART: Yeah – right there (indicates the stomach again).

In a few minutes, Dick was able to reassure the protector who showed up in my stomach that I wouldn't fall apart, and it agreed to let us proceed to the tearful one. But another part, the one I found in my fuzzy head, lodged its own objections.

DICK: See if there are any other **fears** as you contemplate going to this tearful part.
EMMA: My head's going fuzzy now (indicating the back of the head at the base).
DICK: Okay, let's get to know that part that's fuzzing up your brain. (Dick remains accepting, curious and available.)

EMMA: That part's frightened of emotions.
DICK: Ask it about its fear of emotions.
EMMA: They're bad.
DICK: It thinks emotions are bad. (Although Dick uses 'it', he could just as well have used 'you', as the part is quite strongly blended and Dick is really talking to it directly, as he makes clear in a short while.)
EMMA: Scary and bad.
DICK: Ask it where it got that idea from.
EMMA: The big people.
DICK: The big people when you were young gave that message that emotions are bad and scary.
EMMA: Mm (nodding). Yes.
DICK: Okay, so how do you **feel toward** that part now, Emma?
EMMA: (Long pause.) I still feel the pull of the part, quite strongly.
DICK: Okay. You feel quite blended with it.
EMMA: Yes, quite blended with it.
DICK: So let me talk directly with it also.
EMMA: Okay.
DICK: The big people told you emotions were scary and bad. Is that right?
FUZZY PART: I think they showed.
DICK: Oh?
FUZZY PART: They showed.

It's not unusual for parts to want to be accurately understood and because Dick has access to Self-energy, he doesn't take it personally and feel corrected. He continues to be open and interested.

DICK: So, when they got emotional it got scary and bad?

Dick tries to understand more fully from the very little my part is giving away; it's as though he senses that putting things into words for the part is helping it form and find its own words for what is emerging into expression for the first time ever in this dialogue.

FUZZY PART: There was that and there was the fact that ... um ... they fought so hard not to get emotional. Like they would be destroyed if they got emotional.
DICK: OK. So, they showed a lot of fear of emotions.
FUZZY PART: Yes.

DICK: They did their best to stay away from them.

FUZZY PART: Yes (nodding).

DICK: So, I can certainly understand then that would make you worry that emotions are very scary

FUZZY PART: Mm hmm. (The part is in agreement, it feels understood.)

In time, this protector, like the one we attended to earlier, **unblends** and gives us permission to approach the tearful part we began with.

> ### Unblending
> As a reminder: When a part who is overwhelming the Self ceases doing so, we say it has *unblended*. As parts willingly pull their energy back, and allow Self's presence, access to Self-qualities is possible. When parts let Self drive the psychic bus by unblending, we may feel internal spaciousness, calm, openness and curious presence.

Time travel: updating parts

As you might notice from Dick's questions, *curiosity* is at the heart of how IFS works. Noticing trailheads, doing a You-turn, and the process of befriending all take curiosity. But 'curious' can also mean singular, unusual, odd or strange. The next part of the demonstration, where Dick updates a part of me, is certainly curious in that sense.

One of the strangest, yet most useful things we can do when we meet a part is to go all *Doctor Who* on them. Yes, curiously, IFS involves time travel of a sort! You see, parts – whether protectors or exiles – are usually stuck some time in our past, while you (and I) have continued journeying through time to today. *Updating* is the process by which we help the part understand this dual existence across time:

- While their time has remained frozen or stuck, in the outside world time has continued to move on.
- They did in fact survive whatever danger or hurt happened at that time.
- They are protecting the system from that danger or hurt on the inside.
- The part now exists on the inside at one age, while the system as a whole also exists in the outside world at another, older age.
- The grown-up system they are part of has resources, experiences and aspects of identity of which they probably have no awareness.
- There is an ageless Self inside who wants to see, know and love them.

I almost think of updating as the Self's way of introducing itself to the part. But the metaphor isn't quite right. When I introduce myself at an outer-world gathering, it is easy to spot if the person I am introducing myself to is aware of me, listening and interested in getting to meet me (or not). On the inside, by contrast, parts can be so taken up in and by their individual inner reality that they not only fail to notice the passage of time, but they can also fail to notice Self. In 'Parenting from the Inside' (Foot and Redfern, 2023), Anna Vincentz and Joel Bubbers write about how protectors are so busy trying to keep exiles out of consciousness that they 'revolve' around them instead of revolving around Self. Similarly, parts can *choose* not to notice Self's curious presence; they may be used to being alone and in control, or simply too cautious to trust an apparently well-meaning stranger.

At this stage it's always useful to check on the 'hook-up': the term for whether the part you're trying to befriend is aware of your Self and open to knowing it and being known. If I'm guiding someone exploring on the inside, I'll suggest they are curious about the part's awareness of Self using questions like these:

- Do you get a feeling the part senses you are there?
- Can the part feel that curiosity or compassion, welcome and acceptance, and so forth?
- Is eye contact possible between you?
- Is the part open to you being with it right now?
- How close is the part to you?

The answers to these questions will determine your response. If the part is not aware of your Self, it might need patience and time to allow the part to acclimatize to a new presence. Or there may be another part interfering, in which case you can get curious about its need to do that.

The process of befriending a part is like the process of befriending another person: we cannot predict or know in advance the response a part might make. This uncertainty can feel scary to other parts of us, but Self has clarity and confidence in how to respond. A part might respond to Self's curious presence with confusion, fear, anger or something else. If a part is angry that Self has been absent till now, I might suggest sharing with the part an apology: 'I'm sorry I've not come to see you before this, I'd like to get to meet you now if that's okay with you.' For a part holding confusion, I might respond, 'I can see this is confusing, there's no rush. We can take our time getting to know each other.' For a part showing a fearful response, I might want to differentiate Self from others who might have scared it in the past. I might say to the part, 'It makes sense you would be wary; I'm new to you, yet I might look familiar too. I just want to explain that I'm not like the people in the past who have hurt you, I'd like a chance to demonstrate that and earn your trust.'

To all parts stuck in dangerous and distressing circumstances, be sure to tell them that they did indeed survive. After all, you are who they became! Even better, you are also much more than just an older version of one part or another. There are multitudes inside, as well as the timeless Self-energy your parts are just now becoming aware of. You might want to remind them that now they are not alone, that if they (and other parts) give space, the you-who's-not-a-part can be with them.

One of the most wonderful aspects of the updating process is giving your parts a look round your grown-up world. You suggest to the part that, if it's willing, it might enjoy having a look around your current life, which is quite unlike the fearful past it has been trapped in. You aren't stuck in the scene they are stuck in – which can offer hope that they, too, can leave the past and move to be with your Self in the present. Your part might be astonished at the conditions of your life. Imagine how it feels for a young part of you to learn that you're married, or a parent yourself, or have four-legged family members, or a job or a car. Time and personhood have continued into the present day, and – if it wants to – your part will get to inhabit the world of unimagined marvels you now live in.

Naturally, it is important for the part to distinguish your Self from your own parents or past authority figures. If a part is distressed that you resemble your mother, you might say, 'I get that I look just like Ma, but I'm not her, and I'm here to take care of you now.' Or it might feel natural for your Self to talk about your adult body in the third person: 'I get how Emma looks just like Ma, but she's not. Ma died a while back and left us some money we spent on training in IFS. That's how I'm meeting Emma's parts, like you.' Updating using this third-person perspective helps parts understand that your grown-up body is not *all* of who you are. Updating parts about their 'adult self' is not *equating* the 'adult self' with capital-S Self. The part you are meeting with gets to understand there are these *two* resources available now: current-age Emma, the grown-up embodiment of your being in the present, *and* the Emma-who's-not-a-part, who is your ageless Self.

Updating in action

Here is how Dick updated a part of me during our demonstration session – the protective part who made my stomach feel
funny. That protective part was concerned that I'd be too fragile
to withstand the feelings of the tearful part we'd started with:

DICK (addressing the part): Okay, and how old do you think she is?
GUT PART: 'She'?
DICK: Yes, how old is Emma?
GUT PART (grinning): Mm. I want to say, 'The real Emma you mean?'
(By this the part meant the flesh-and-blood 3D Emma.)
DICK: Uh huh.
GUT PART: Yes, yes, she's 51.
DICK: Okay, that's fine, but—
GUT PART (interrupting): But little Emma's like this big. (I show a hand-
ful size, cupping both hands in front of me.)
DICK: The tearful one or the you I'm talking to?
GUT PART: Not me.
DICK: So, the one you were wanting to go to at some point.
GUT PART: Possibly.
DICK: Okay, very small and very fragile. So, you're really convinced
she would disintegrate if you went there?
GUT PART: I'm not as convinced now; I'm not as scared now.
DICK: Okay, good, do you know why?
GUT PART: I think just being able to say it.
DICK: That's right. That's great. So, would you be willing to let us go
to the tearful one so we can heal it? And I can promise you she won't
disintegrate?
GUT PART: Yes.

I'm pretty sure from this distance that the updating process
is what helped this part's fear ease up. The awareness that the
fragile, tearful Emma had survived and reached 51 years of age
was powerful reassurance.

Once that part withdrew its objections, Dick returned to the
other protector who had shown up in fuzziness at the back of
my head to update it as well.

> DICK: And how old do you think Emma is?
>
> FUZZY PART: She's old, she's an old lady (laughing). She's an old lady.

Some fear has diminished for this part, too, making space for some playfulness – one of the Ps of Self-leadership – and perspective.

> DICK (laughing too): Okay, but you still don't think she can handle emotions?
>
> FUZZY PART: Um, I think *she* can, I'm not so sure about some of the parts.
>
> DICK: Which parts are you worried about in particular?
>
> FUZZY PART: The littler parts.
>
> DICK: Okay, alright. Well, how about if we had Emma go to those littler parts so they wouldn't have to handle them [emotions] by themselves? (The fuzzy part nods my head, visibly emotional.) Does that work for you?
>
> EMMA (still visibly emotional, but back in my Self): Now I'm getting in touch with some sad.
>
> DICK: Is it okay? Just check if it's okay with everybody. (I nod.) That's great. How do you feel toward the sad part?
>
> EMMA: Welcoming. (Dick recognizes this is my Self again: welcoming is one of the AWOLs of Self-energy.)
>
> DICK: Wonderful. So, let's do welcome it and see what it wants you to know about itself.
>
> EMMA: It wants me to know how big the sad is.
>
> DICK: Is it okay to know that?
>
> EMMA: Yes.

I'll share more from our demonstration session in the next chapter.

The importance of consent

The previous excerpt highlights another important aspect of IFS: we are scrupulous about asking protectors for permission to go to the more wounded parts that they protect. Now, you may be thinking, how does one get consent in a system of multiple sentient beings? What a great question that is! As best you can, moment to moment, and part by part. When doing IFS, protectors can give us their permission to enquire inside, relax and allow the Self-to-part relationships to unfold. *And* they can return and exert control again if they are uncertain or fearful, at any point, for any reason. We negotiate with them, hear and understand them, address any concern or need they have in the moment, and then we renew our request for permission to continue.[2]

Asking for consent makes a world of difference inside. Remember, parts can often be the age of children and teenagers, who often resent being told what to do by adults. And their caution about internal exploration makes sense in the light of their circumstances. In the world our parts inhabit, there is often a heightened perception of threat, a sense of a lack of available resources, and a rigid vigilance. There can also be a deeply ingrained fear of intimacy, vulnerability, emotions and relational connection. When our Self asks for permission to get to know a part, it *always* takes no for an answer.

The importance of consent is a significant way in which inner Self-leadership is different from the leadership of an external family. In the inner world, parts give space for and move aside for Self, which does not dictate or *make* parts step aside. I doubt many external parents seek permission all the time from their children for every little thing. But when a child is upset, approaching them with respect and acknowledging their boundaries and choices is fundamental. As without, so within.

Parenting: Befriending on the inside to connect on the outside

IFS colleagues Anna Vincentz and Joel Bubbers have written a detailed, warts-and-all, touching and inspiring chapter in *Freeing Self: IFS beyond the Therapy Room* (Foot and Redfern, 2023). Here is an example from 'Parenting from the inside' (pp. 246–8) of Anna befriending and leading her own system as she connects with her child.

[B]ecoming aware of our own internal landscape one step at a time, makes a big difference. We can (more often) stop reacting *from* burdened parts and become more Self-led in our parenting, thereby being secure attachment figures for the parts of our inner children that have felt unsafe and unloved. We can then start creating the strong connections to our own children that feel secure for them to grow up in and that we all long for as human beings [...]

My daughter, 9 years old now, doesn't want to go to school today. She's trying to hide in bed under the covers and both her body language and words are aggressive: 'No! I am not going to school!'

Even though I am more relaxed, more present, a part instantly shows up with an internal 'Oh no, not this again!'

Healing our inner dynamics and burdens takes time and has many layers so when the trigger is there, the same parts will often show up, perhaps with less force, but the difference is (with practice and awareness) that we start to notice them (sooner).

As soon as I become aware of the part, I slow myself down and start focusing inwards. I know that either I am in relation to this part from the inside or this part will be leading the way in relation to my daughter, which is not what I want and not what she needs. I turn my attention inwards to be with the part without trying to change anything about it and I also take time to notice mySelf inside. I do this by noticing my breath, making it conscious and deep, expanding the space in my chest and stomach, and especially, with every breath inward focusing in on my heart till it feels (just a little) warmer and more open to whatever is going on inside and outside of me. I feel myself and my body more fully from the inside; I feel more grounded and rooted in the world and in the present.

The part is much easier to distinguish from the rest of me now. I notice the words once more, 'Oh no, not this again!' and get an image of this part literally trying to stay afloat on the surface of a deep ocean, always close to sinking under. Always struggling. My stomach and throat tighten up at seeing the image, and a deep despair and hopelessness feels ready to consume me. I know that this comes from the exile hidden away underneath.

From my open heart and grounded breath, I let the part (and the pain from the exile underneath) know that I notice them; that I am here. And I invite what is there to notice me as well, to notice my open heart. I check with the part what it needs, to be able to give me some space.

All of our parts have stories, and this part already said a lot in the image it showed me. It already makes a lot of sense even if I might not know the exact narrative behind it. The here and now connection is enough for the time being; I promise to return. ...

As the part gives space, I still have it in my consciousness – it is still there – but it is not blended in the same way and is able to inform me instead of being in the lead.

As I focus outwards again, I feel calmer, and I ask my daughter if it is okay that I sit down next to her on the bed. She nods from under the covers, and I sit down quietly. At this moment I don't have any agenda other than meeting her where she is. This does not mean that I don't care if she goes to school or not, but that right now, that is not what matters the most. When she can feel from me that I am not trying to get her to come out, she relaxes a little and I ask if she wants to come sit with me. She crawls up on my lap and we just hug quietly for some time. When she lets go a little from the hug, I let her know that I see and hear her. That I am here.

'I can see that you don't want to get out of bed because you don't want to go to school. Is that right?' She nods, so I continue: 'And I can imagine how difficult or unfair it must feel being you right now, so you say "No, I don't want to go and you cannot make me!" Because you so wish that you could stay home. Is that how it is for you right now?'

'Yes,' she answers, 'Can't I just stay home today?'

'I know you really want to stay home. I can hear that.'

'Can I?'

'No. I want you to go to school.'

You can hear Anna guessing at parts active inside her daughter – but she asks what they are feeling, rather than presuming to know. Just as importantly, Anna's Self-led care for her own inner family enables her to care for her daughter:

Because I have slowed down and become curious about myself, I am (more) unblended from my triggered parts. And because I am more unblended from my triggered parts, I am able to slow down and become curious about my daughter and be there in the way she needs me to be. This helps me connect with her from the inside; from a Self-led space where she can feel exactly as she does and still feel loved and connected.

If you are a parent or caregiver, does this account inspire you? Does it seem realistic to you? Or does a part dismiss it, wondering, *And how many times did her daughter go to school after all, I'd like to know?* This sceptical part is welcome – as is any part who wants to get the child to school for fear of what life in the future might be like for her otherwise. Maybe you could experiment with Anna's approach yourself: ask parts to give you space to connect with your child without agenda, and be with their system as it is. On some days your child's parts, having felt seen, heard and welcomed, might calm and become able to attend school. On other days, you might choose clearly and consciously that attendance is not in their best interest.

Journal prompt

Practising updating

To prepare for what you might encounter inside, I propose you get curious about what you might say to a young child part inside of you when you meet for the first time. Consider what resources you have now that you didn't have when you were younger. How has life changed for you – and therefore potentially for your inner family – for the better? Large changes, like being free from an abusive situation, might make a big impression. But apparently inconsequential features of your adult life might be quite as moving: you might have young parts who are delighted that you are as tall as you are, or who marvel that you can drive a car.

5

Healing an exile with support

In this chapter I take you deeper into the therapeutic healing that is available when using more of the Internal Family Systems model with expert support. That's what happened for me during the session Dick Schwartz facilitated for my system back in 2016.

The steps of healing

Once Self is accessible and available inside, and after moving through the 6 Fs, burdened parts of us can be healed. Over time, IFS practitioners have described the process Self uses for healing as:

- witnessing
- redo or do-over
- retrieval
- unburdening
- invitation
- integration and appreciation.

Figure 5.1 is a way of visualizing these steps. You may remember a drawing of an 'inner child' in Chapter 1 – that young one had their head down and seemed very alone. When the Self is there to *witness* that child's experience, they can lift their head up: someone is with them, listening. The heart surrounds this inner child to represent the presence of Self-energy.

The clapperboard shows how the Self, like a movie director, can *redo* the scene the exile is trapped in, until the action is exactly as it should be. There is a truism in most forms of therapy that *you can't change the past* – but in IFS and other transformational approaches, you can! Take two, anyone?

The third image clearly shows an open, unbarred exit. This is to signify that the Self of the inner world can go back into the past to the part who is stuck there – *retrieving* the part from an unsafe place and time to the security of the here and now, if that's what the part wants.

On the way from the past to the present, the Self helps the part *unburden* itself of the false beliefs that have kept it trapped in the past. IFS practitioners find that parts usually want to consign the burden, in a physical form, to one of the ancient elements: light, earth, air, water or fire. When a part unburdens to fire, for example, a bonfire is often built in imagination, and the part, with assistance from Self, releases or lets go of the burden it has been carrying and surrenders it to the flames.

Once the burden is gone, there's space in the part for something else, a belief about its goodness and worth. The penultimate image is of a special, sparkly, exciting gift to represent the qualities that parts who have unburdened then *invite* into themselves for the life ahead.

Finally, a 'Welcome Home' banner: *integration*. When a burdened part returns to the inner family in the here and now, full of positive qualities, it can often feel like a homecoming and celebration. Under the banner, every part welcomes the unburdened one into the fold, expressing joyful *appreciation* for its courage and positive qualities.

Not all steps are relevant in every case, and protectors can often let go of their burdens without going through the whole process. For our exiles, unburdening limiting beliefs, leaving memories and places they are trapped in, and having inner do-overs lets these inner little ones reclaim their inherently valuable, joyful, open natures – but leaving the past requires them to take a harrowing leap of faith: that the

Witnessing

Redo

Retrieval

Unburdening

Invitation

Integration

Figure 5.1 Steps of healing

present will be better, and that Self will always love them. In Self's presence, exiles usually need to make their way through all the steps, sometimes more than once, and it is wise to enlist the support of a trained IFS professional before you attempt to heal them.

Witnessing

Continuing to share the session I had with Dick Schwartz, you may recall that in the previous chapter, he had reassured a couple of protectors, who had given their permission for me to approach the tearful part I was curious about. Now, as my Self focuses on that part, Dick leads me to *witness* its experience.

> EMMA: It wants me to know how big the sad is.
> DICK: Is it okay to know that?
> EMMA: Yes.
> DICK: So let it know that you get that it's very big.
> EMMA (nodding): I get it's very big.
> DICK: Yes. What else does it want you to know about itself?
> EMMA: It's very loud.
> DICK: Is it okay that it's very loud? (Dick is checking that parts haven't been activated by the noise to come back in and constrain Self's presence. It's not a problem, Self is still present and curious. I nod in answer to his question.) So let it know, it's fine. (I nod once more.) Is it saying something loud or is it screaming?
> EMMA: It's not got words.
> DICK: Just kind of loud emotion?
> EMMA: Yes.
> DICK: Okay. What else does it want you to know about itself?
> EMMA: It's full, the part seems to be full of water.
> DICK: Full of sadness?
> EMMA: Full of water.
> DICK: Okay. It's full of water.

This is a really great example of holding the principle of not knowing and not assuming. Instead, we ask, and are curious. The founder of IFS himself voiced that 'water' meant *sadness*, but my part swiftly corrected him, and he accepted the correction immediately.

> DICK: See what it wants you to know about that water.
> EMMA: It's like the sea.
> DICK: Uh huh. In the sense that it's very vast.
> EMMA: Yes.

Now, you may notice that Dick is offering suggestions here ('very vast'), which might seem to go against the IFS maxim of *just ask*. So, let me explain: I see this as 'loud empathy'.[1] When two people are immersed in Self-energy like this, it's almost as though we join the same energetic or spiritual field – I don't know what else to call it – and the facilitator or therapist often 'knows' in an experiential sense what is going on inside the other in the common field. This isn't the same as head knowledge, and it's hard to explain. What's important is that, even if Dick (or another therapist or IFS person) is picking something up, it's not imposed, it's proposed as a possibility. And in this case I confirm that Dick has understood correctly: yes, very vast.

> DICK: How do you feel toward it now knowing that it carries all this water?
> EMMA: Open.
> DICK: So let it know you're still welcoming and open and what else does it want you to know about all that.
> EMMA: It's very, very alone.
> DICK: Uh huh.
> EMMA: And watched.
> DICK: Mm hmm. (Do you see how Dick remains present, no need to reflect the words I used back to me every time? He's getting what I'm sharing and I'm getting him getting me.)
> EMMA: And it's like, it's frightening to other people.
> DICK: Mm hmm. Yes. So, people are watching.
> EMMA: Yes, people are watching and it's, it's separate from everybody.
> DICK: Yeah, and whenever it starts to show itself, they get frightened, is that right?
> EMMA: I think so, there's a frozen, freezing element.
> DICK: They freeze.
> EMMA: I think so, yes.
> DICK: Just ask if that's true. (Dick has made a suggestion, and in the spirit of curiosity he reminds me to check it out directly with the part.)
> EMMA: Yes, that's what it experiences, everybody is freezing around it.
> DICK: What's it like for this part?
> EMMA: Scary.

> DICK: Very scary. Is it okay for you to know about that?
> EMMA: Yes.

I so appreciate that of all that I've shared, Dick reflected that piece back: 'very scary'. Through my whole early life fear was taboo; there was perpetual fear *of* the fear. This mutual recognition and witnessing of the fear felt very special. When he asks, 'Is it okay?', Dick wants to check that no parts are upset by this enquiry, and that Self has not been displaced. Self in me is still present.

> DICK: So let it know it's okay for you to know how scary it was to be around these freezing people.
> EMMA (After a long pause): And it soothes itself.
> DICK: How does it do that?
> EMMA: Like the sea ... like the sea soothes.
> DICK: Helps it not need the people so much.
> EMMA: Yes.
> DICK: That makes sense?
> EMMA: Yes.
> DICK: So let it know you get that.

I now live ten miles from the sea and love the sound, feel, colour, grandeur of it, though not its saltiness in my mouth and nose when I swim! As I write this now a decade later, I am still moved by this experience and saddened.

Let me add some context. My twin sister and I were born prematurely in the 1960s. Requiring a variety of emergency procedures including a blood transfusion for me, we were placed in separate incubators where we stayed for six weeks. It's always been my sense that this session relates to that very early trauma in some way and heals aspects of it, though there is much still to heal. You'll see what I mean as Dick moves on to the next healing step, the do-over.

Redo

In this powerful and liberating step, in the presence of Self, the past can be altered in any way the part wishes, in any way that organically needs to happen. In imagination, Self can go back to where the exile is stuck and be with it exactly in the way it needed someone to be with it back then. Also, in Self's presence, the part can have a do-over in terms of how it did or didn't act. The part can experience just being in the presence of Self as a do-over, an experience of being accompanied and held rather than left to endure trauma all alone.

The difference between the two worlds, inner and outer, is intuitively clear in practice, but, as you read this, you might be a bit confused. To explain, experiencing a redo on the inside will never change what actually happened, the outer-world facts do not change, but the emotional experiencing of them does.

Beyond IFS, other therapeutic approaches have similar outcomes (Ecker et al., 2024). For example, my parts and I clearly recall the events of the day my flat burned down, which include going down a fireman's ladder sobbing hysterically. But after working with the memory using eye movement desensitization and reprocessing (EMDR) therapy, the emotional charge linked to those horrifying events is gone. IFS offers more expansive therapeutic possibilities than EMDR, in my experience, because of its emphasis on the presence of Self. On the inside, anything is possible in the presence of Self. I have witnessed parts and Self redo the past in breathtaking ways:

- A part rescues itself, its mother and sibling from an abuser.
- A part that the system thought was dead comes back to life.
- A part punches and kicks to escape being kidnapped, jabbing and lashing out with the present-day body's arms and hands.
- A part learns that it wasn't at fault or in any way responsible for their parent leaving the family home.

The authors of 'Embodying IFS with Native American Clients' describe this inside-world experience exquisitely:

> I told Little One that in the magical alternative IFS universe, anything is possible. It is like a portal into a place where people, time, and materials manifest exactly as we need

them. It takes some practice to believe this is true. And once you know it is, there's no going back. Creativity becomes a positive reinforcing spiral loop of manifestation. (Sullivan et al., 2023, p. 212)

Spontaneously, in the demonstration session with Dick, just such a redo is beginning to happen:

> EMMA: There's a hand coming out of it [the water] now.
> DICK: Good, let it know that it's safe to reach out.
> EMMA (after a long pause): I feel drawn to it.
> DICK: Great, so can you get close to it?
> EMMA: I'm telling it I'm here.
> DICK: That's great. How's it reacting?
> EMMA (shaking my head): It's not, it feels like I can't get closer.

The water is gradually becoming a person, or personifying – and a protective part has come in who wants me to stay away from it:

> DICK: Why's that?
> EMMA: It says she's not ready.
> DICK: Because why?
> EMMA: I'm hearing the words 'She's too early' coming.
> DICK: Ask it what it means by that.
> EMMA: Born too early.
> DICK: Too early for what?
> EMMA: To be healthy.
> DICK: Is this making sense to you, Emma? (Dick doesn't have to understand exactly what my part means, in the moment or ever, but it's important that *I* understand and can communicate that to the protective part.)
> EMMA: Yes, I get it, and I get that, and I know that. I get it.
> DICK: Okay, what do you say to the part about that?
> EMMA: I get it, I know it, and that's how it is and that's how it was, but she [the water-part] still needs ... she still needs us, and she needs me, and there's nothing to be afraid of.
> DICK: Exactly.
> EMMA (sigh): That part's stepping back now.
> DICK: That's great.
> EMMA (reaching out my left hand, clasping something but letting it drop): Another part is coming in – it doesn't believe something; it doesn't believe that I can reach her.

DICK: What do you say to that?
EMMA: I've done it before somehow.
DICK: OK, what does the part say?
EMMA: It's scared, it's scared of something, of failing – the process failing.

Many protective and alarmed parts interrupt now, and Dick gains permission to speak to the parts directly, which seems to be their preference. (This is why many of us in the IFS community suggest deep inner work is best done accompanied by an IFS professional.) I list the parts here for your information and then highlight a couple of important points:

- One passionately asserts that I have the right to fail.
- Another critical one just knows I *will* fail at this.
- A part is angry at the critical part.
- Another says therapy is all mumbo-jumbo and never fully heals anything.
- One more part is frightened that we will all drown in the sadness the water-part holds.

As Dick talks with the parts to address their fears, further redoing is taking place for them as well. Once all the protectors agree to let us proceed, we move ahead to the next part of the process: retrieving my exiled water-part from the lonely past.

Retrieval

When a part is ready, and not a moment before, Self helps it move across time and space to escape where it has been stuck in the past. It may come and be with Self and rejoin the system in the present; sometimes a part will prefer to go to an imaginary place of its choice instead. The part always knows where it wants to be: perhaps a hideout in the woods, an encampment on the beach, a person's cosy bedroom, safe inside their heart.

An exile's decision to allow itself to be retrieved from the past is momentous for the whole system, and sometimes other parts will intervene – often because they don't trust Self to keep the exile safe. In this case, what IFS calls a **Self-like part** subtly displaced my Self.

> DICK: How does it feel now to get closer to the sadness?
> EMMA: It's changed. She's up stone steps, in like a font, a baptismal font, the water and the hand.
> DICK: How close are you to her? (Dick may have sensed a disturbance in my Self-energy; he is checking on the hook-up.)
> EMMA: There's another part closer to her, looking down on her, seeing you and me in the chair.
> DICK: In the chair, how close are you?
> EMMA: Quite close. I see all that and yet I feel like I'm in the chair.
> DICK: You can see you in the chair?
> EMMA: Yes.
> DICK: OK, so what I'd like is for you to actually be there so you can't see yourself. (I open my eyes to reconnect with Dick.) You don't see yourself because you're there; is that possible?
> EMMA (closing my eyes again): I can feel me and see me at the same time.
> DICK: The you you can feel is the one we want to be there.
> EMMA: Okay.

Self-like parts

Self-like parts tend to want to believe they are Self and that they must lead the system. Ideally, an IFS professional won't overreact but validate and appreciate the part for its efforts on behalf of the system. Negotiating an introduction to Self is important; Self-like parts are often willing to assist or partner with Self, given the opportunity to do so. Like other parts, they do not have the same transformational and leadership abilities that Self has.

> DICK: How do you feel toward the font part? How close are you?

Dick is demonstrating how it is important to recheck Self's presence and availability once a protector – the Self-like part – gives space. Checking on proximity tests the hook-up, or how the part is receiving or welcoming Self's presence – although, at the time,

I respond about how I am feeling towards the part in between me and the font part:

EMMA: Open. Close.
DICK: Let it know.
EMMA: I'm grateful to it.
DICK: Good, let it know that too.
EMMA: It's keeping her [the exile] safe. (Notice how to Self all parts are welcome, all parts are valued – even ones trying to 'do Self's job' or usurp Self in a way.)
DICK: How do you feel toward her, the water and the hand? (Dick returns our attention to the chosen part.)
EMMA: Tender. (Tenderness is much like compassion, so Dick can tell that my Self is back in the **seat of consciousness**.)
DICK: Let her know.
EMMA: I want to get to know her better. (The Emma-who's-not-a-part wants to connect and be with the chosen part.)
DICK: Let her know that too.
EMMA: I feel like I want to have her come be with me.
DICK: Invite her to do that.
EMMA: The part gave her to me.
DICK: Great, how are you being with her?
EMMA: Gentle.
DICK: How is she reacting?
EMMA: She's looking up at me and knows you're there as well; she feels safe.
DICK: That's right, she's totally safe. How does that feel to her, to feel safe?
EMMA: She's not water anymore, she's flesh and blood.
DICK: Yes, she's—
EMMA (interrupting): She's not broken, she's whole ... (The redo is continuing through the part's new relationship with Self.)

The seat of consciousness

When we are in the inner world, we see through the eyes of Self. If in our mind's eye we see ourselves as we are today, that suggests the presence of a protector who may be trying to take the place of Self for its own reasons. Some protectors are quite practised at playing the role of Self, so it takes some skill to notice when this happens. When it does, we can ask the Self-like part to unblend to allow Self to come alongside and befriend it.

Unburdening

Once the exiled part has moved from the past to a safe place, Self helps the part let go of the burdens it has been carrying. Burdens, if you recall, are beliefs that cause suffering, but in the imaginary realm inside they often take physical form, in, on or around a part's body: a coating of sludge, a heavy tumour, a cloud of smoke, or the like. Self helps the part get hold of its burdens and, when all is ready, the part ceremoniously or ritually releases them to one of the elements – air, earth, fire, light, water – in a way that feels right for it.

Sometimes you will find burdens that are personal (from experience), legacy (handed down from a previous generation), cultural, or a mixture of all three. In this case, it unfolds that some of my part's sadness is a legacy burden. Dick helps me address my part's fear that the relationship with a primary caregiver will change for the worse if the legacy burden is released. Once that objection has been resolved, Dick knows my part is ready to let go of her burden:

> DICK: Let her know that you're gonna be taking care of her now. How would it feel now to send this out of your body?
> EMMA: Good.
> DICK: What would she like to give it up to?
> EMMA: Wind.
> DICK: Out and off your body. Let the wind carry it away.
> EMMA (blowing) … Now we're doing light as well.
> DICK: Let it all go to the light and the wind.
> EMMA: I think the broken's all gone.
> DICK: Just check to be sure it's all gone.
> EMMA: Maybe not all the broken.
> DICK: We're gonna wait till it's all gone. (Dick is demonstrating two of the 5 Ps, patience and persistence.)
> EMMA: Does it *all* need to go? (There's a lingering concern about what might happen without the sadness, but Dick responds with confidence.)
> DICK: Yes, of course … No rush. How's she doing?
> EMMA: She's great.
> DICK: How's your body feeling?
> EMMA: Relaxed.

Invitation

When a part is unburdened, we invite it to fill up the space the unburdening has created with qualities it would like or will need in the future, or qualities that were formerly squashed down or pushed out by the burden. Again, the part will know what qualities it wants to invite: peace, fun and play are popular.

> DICK: You and she can invite qualities in if you like.
> EMMA: Playful.
> DICK: Tell her to invite that into her body.
> EMMA: She's cheeky, very, very cheeky ... and free flowing ... and soft ... and whole. (I recall the invitation came with water, I could see her and the Self-like part playing joyfully in a shower of water.)
> DICK: Does she want to hang out with you now or go someplace else?
> EMMA: Wants to hang out with me.

The invitation is complete, and my formerly tearful exile has exchanged vast sadness for playfulness. Now Dick initiates the next healing step, integration.

Integration and appreciation

Unburdening can create major transformational shifts in the system, so taking time and care to integrate the changes internally and externally is important. At this point Self invites key and relevant protectors, especially those who may have expressed concerns during the process, to notice what has just happened. Fears and concerns of any part may need to be addressed, and it's wise to put plans in place with the exile to check in on them every day for up to a month. This is also an opportunity for any protectors to change their role or go through unburdening for themselves.

To be clear, 'integration' does not mean that parts must grow up to your current chronological age, nor does it mean that parts 'dissolve' back into the Self. Yes, some parts may be less active once they've let go of their burdens (off playing on the beach of their choice, for example) – but none will be lost or got rid of. Remember, every part of your inner family is indispensable:

> DICK: Bring in all the parts … who didn't think this could happen to see what she's like now.
> EMMA (smiling): She's waving.
> DICK: How are they reacting?
> EMMA: Curious.
> DICK: Tell them to really check it out.
> EMMA: They feel like they're united in it, in meeting her.
> DICK: They can all think about new roles, the one who wants to make you laugh can start doing that …
> EMMA: The one that kept all the bad stuff out can start letting the good stuff in.
> DICK: Exactly, like love …
> EMMA: The big angry one feels different as well, more protective.
> DICK: That's great. How's it feeling in general in there now?
> EMMA: Calm, it just feels more like a family with a new baby that's being welcomed.
> DICK: That's sort of like what it is.
> EMMA: I've got their backs, and they can help, they all do.
> DICK: Tell them they can trust you to lead this family now.

This moment demonstrates one of the goals of IFS: in my system, Self-leadership is possible and desirable. Self spontaneously understands and communicates what this means.

> DICK: Does that feel complete for now, Emma?
> EMMA: They've just moved to a new configuration. I want to be with that just a tiny while.
> DICK: That's fine.
> EMMA: Yeah.

I also like to think of **appreciation** as a separate step all by itself. Just as in families in the external world, appreciation goes a long way to build trust and cooperation; it is important to spend time appreciating parts who made space for another part's healing. Perhaps an exile agreed to wait while another one was tended to, or protectors trusted enough to step back and let Self take the lead. Appreciation is valuable from Self to parts all of whom serve the system in the ways that they do, and between parts even who by virtue of belonging to the same system find themselves 'on the same team'. I believe my parts felt my appreciation when I said, 'they can help, they all do'.

Appreciation

Offering appreciation and being grateful towards parts acts in the inner system like oil does in a machine, smoothing the way. A regular practice of gratitude and appreciation towards other people's parts also eases connection and communication but can be harder to come by.

Journal prompt

Reflecting on the healing steps

Here are some reflection questions on this chapter for you to consider alone, with a reading partner if you have one, or in your book club or IFS reading group.

- Did the images for the healing steps work for your system? If not, what images would you use to encapsulate each step?
- If you have had therapy before, do you recognize anything similar to these IFS healing steps?
- Did anyone inside react strongly to a particular healing step? If so, can you be curious and find out more?
- How are you feeling as you come to the end of this section of the book? Are your parts ready to move on? If not, what might they need or want from the you-who's-not-a-part for now?

Section 3
USING IFS YOURSELF

6

Nurturing internal relationships by attending to fear

As you experiment with IFS, you might find yourself noticing your parts with greatest clarity when they're afraid of something. That makes all the sense in the world, because the protective parts of our internal families are dedicated to preventing us from coming to harm in the ways we have in the past. In a sense, our burdened protectors live in fear, and they perform heroic feats to keep the outcomes they fear from coming to pass. Our managers arrange our lives with infinite care to keep us from dangerous situations; when they fail, our firefighters spring into action to keep the scary emotions of our exiles safely out of our awareness. For that reason, being attentive to our parts' fears is a powerful way into inner enquiry.

In this chapter, I'll share two case studies that centre on fear: one person's mild fear of driving, another's extreme fear of snakes. In both cases, the fear opens up the opportunity for inner healing through IFS. But first, because fear is a potent feeling, I want to talk about how to cultivate an IFS practice for yourself that will enable you to handle fear safely.

Ways of working with fear
Making space, creating rituals and starting gently

Are you making space for IFS in your busy life and schedule? If not, when might work for you? My system prefers mornings, so journalling first thing or going out for a walk (weather permitting) are times when I can hear from and connect with my parts. You might like to journal at night as part of a night-time routine. Perhaps you are content to contact and slow down to listen to parts when they make themselves known in times of crisis. Or you might be interested in the *idea* of IFS, but still not quite ready to explore your own inner world. It can take a while to go from routinely ignoring, numbing, pushing away, and taking for granted our parts (as Western modern society encourages), to actively embracing inner multiplicity at any level. Go easy and gently if you can. Having an intention to create space for connection can encourage your parts to become more apparent to you; looking out for opportunities can bring them into even clearer view.

You can get started with IFS without making special time for it, if you'd rather. Perhaps you can include internal connecting and relationship-building in something you already do. How about next time you go to the gym you get curious: Who wants to be here? Who struggles with this and wants to cancel but gets overridden? Or maybe a public place isn't right for you to think about your inner world. Perhaps you could build a little time into your schedule when you are comfortably alone, and you can 'just be'. To drop into yourself in a ritualized way, slowing down and opening up to what's there. You may already have a regular practice that you can adapt, such as taking the dog out early in the morning in a secluded place, walking on the beach at low tide, or sitting on a roof terrace somewhere up above the world. If so, see if you can make that time sacred or more special, if that appeals to you.

Parts of you might wonder what it feels like to 'drop in' to your inner world. Anna Vincentz and Joel Bubbers explain it well:

> In focusing inward you're not searching for anything on the inside, but simply focusing on your breath, your heart, your inner space, your feelings of being (or not being) grounded and held inside and out. This is about feeling

your Self-energy *and* your parts. Because when you have more space (Self-access) inside, you can better be with whatever parts are present. Access to Self is not something we force into our bodies and minds, but something that opens up (to some extent) when we slow down and become present inside.

Self-energy feels unique to everyone, but it *can* feel like an open and warm heart, like energy flowing, like light inside and out. It can feel like spaciousness, especially in the heart and chest area. It can feel like groundedness and rootedness from the inside. It can also feel like more loving feelings and thoughts in relation to what is going on inside and out, or like the 8 Cs of Self: compassion, creativity, curiosity, confidence, courage, calm, connectedness and clarity. ... If only the smallest amount of space, groundedness and warmth is available at this moment, this is fine too. A little goes a long way. (2023, pp. 251–2)

If you already have some sort of meditation practice, perhaps that can be expanded to include a sense of parts and multiplicity. Someone I know practises *metta bhavana*, Buddhist loving-kindness meditation, and now invites his parts to receive compassion during his meditation time. As a result, he senses there is more space inside of him, less physical tension and less of a sense of wanting that tension gone.

Keeping track

Don't worry if at this stage you don't want to make space or create a ritual for your own IFS work. The last thing I want is to help you create more 'shoulds' and 'musts' in life. But if you have developed a practice of some kind, I encourage you to keep track of it – not rigidly, but in some way that feels easy and right for your system.

If you need some ideas, think back to times before day-to-day responsibility. Maybe in the back of an exercise book or in a scrapbook you created photo collages of things and people that were important to you and who you wanted to emulate. Perhaps you stuck posters on the walls of your room. If you are younger than me, you might use social media as a public record of life and living as it unfolds. Well, now you're embracing IFS as a mental health resource and personal exploration tool, see if you can re-awaken those urges to capture important moments and relationships. Just as you might keep track of important dates, names and family relationships in the outside world, why not create a record and keep track of who's who in the inside world?

As you go, remember that IFS is a dynamic process; these are inner relationships you are creating, and relationships are always evolving. It's not that you are memorializing or setting something in stone when you create a record of a part. For example, if you use index cards to record details about parts and their experiences, think of each one as just a snapshot in time. Next time you meet the part, you might want to make a new index card, just as you might take another photo when you next meet an external family member or friend.

Also, did you ever keep a private diary detailing your innermost thoughts, feelings, hopes and dreams? Journalling is a form of what's known as 'externalizing': putting outside of ourselves what we feel and think inside, in this case through writing. Others use drawing or more creative methods, and we'll talk more about those in the next chapter.

Haddon's fear of driving: meeting his protector

Here is a fictionalized case study to further bring IFS to life. (Handy reminders of IFS ideas appear in Table 6.1 below.)

Table 6.1 The 6 Fs, 8 Cs, 5 Ps and AWOLs: A reminder

• **The 6 Fs:** to build a relationship with a protector:
  ◦ Find.
  ◦ Focus.
  ◦ Flesh out.
  ◦ Feel towards – be curious about how you feel towards the part.
  ◦ beFriend the protector, offering a curious, welcoming presence.
  ◦ Fears – address the part's fears and continue to build a trusting relationship.

• **The 8 Cs:** curiosity, creativity, courage, connectedness, confidence, compassion, clarity and calm.
• **The 5 Ps:** patience, persistence, perspective, playfulness, presence.
• **The AWOLs:** acceptance, availability and appreciation; welcome; open heartedness; love.

Haddon, 21, is in the last year of university. We've had sessions together previously, and I remember him fondly. He's coming to me now privately for IFS sessions, as a close friend at another university who benefited from IFS recommended it. Haddon is experiencing anxiety related to driving lessons.

> HADDON: I've been doing extra shifts during the week at the pub where I work to pay for driving lessons. Mr Marshall's a friend of my mum's and he gives me mates' rates, but even so.
> EMMA: Yes, it's an expensive business learning to drive.
> HADDON: Anyway, he picks me up from my student flat on a Sunday after the shops have shut and we go to this empty out of town car park for me to practise. It's been going really well.

Haddon slows to a stop and his slumped body language contradicts his last statement.

> EMMA: It's been going well, but there's more to it?
> HADDON: Yes, now he wants me to go on the road, the *real* road! In my head I'm, *No way!* But I make out that I can't do it as my mum is nervous about me going on the road so soon, and he backs off.
> EMMA: Let me see if I've understood. On the one hand it's going well, your skills are such that your driving instructor thinks you can

progress to having driving lessons on the roads. On the other hand, it seems like a part holding anxiety starts making itself known at even the idea of that.

Haddon is nodding as I speak, but I can tell his brain is in a whirl.

HADDON: Yes, and I'm realizing it's not just the driving lessons either. When I used to walk my sister to school; whenever we crossed the road, I'd hold her hand real tight.

EMMA: That sounds like important information, Haddon. (I pause to see if more is forthcoming; it seems not.) Would you be willing to put your attention inside of you and meet the part with this anxiety about roads?

I invite Haddon to do a You-turn inside; I am guessing that we would do well to meet with a protector with concerns about road safety.

HADDON: Yes, sure. I'm not going to close my eyes or anything, though.

EMMA: That's fine with me. Is it okay if I look at you while I guide you through trying to meet this part?

HADDON: Sure.

He lowers his head and bends forward over his hands which are clasped out in front of him between us. I begin the process of the 6 Fs with him:

EMMA: Now, see if you can find the relevant part somewhere in or around your body ... Where do you sense it?

HADDON: I feel it in my chest (he rubs there gently with one hand), it's tight and my breathing's affected.

EMMA: Ah great noticing; are the sensations tolerable for you now?

HADDON (nods): Now my palms are getting sweaty.' (He's rubbing them on his arms.)

EMMA: Still tolerable for you? (He nods, head still down.) As you notice these sensations, do you get a sense of how old this part might be?

HADDON: I don't see anything, but it feels kind of young. Phew, that's a lot of anxiety it's carrying! But it also feels like it's not the whole of me too.

EMMA: Yes, Haddon, it's not the whole of you, you're right. And as you notice that and this part, how do you feel towards it?'

At the indication that there is some separation between the part and Haddon, I ask the key IFS question to establish the presence or absence of Self:

HADDON: Yeah, okay, I guess. It feels like it's trying to help me. (Haddon instinctively feels the protective nature of the part.)

EMMA: Can you send it some appreciation, Haddon, for communicating with you now and for what it's doing on the inside for you.

HADDON: Mm hmm. (He's rubbing his chest gently; it looks soothing from where I'm sitting.) I'm telling it, I'm here, and ready to listen to what it has to say.

EMMA: Absolutely, and how does it respond?

HADDON: It feels like it softened just a bit – relief, yes, that's what it feels like.

EMMA: Notice that, and when it feels right, ask this part what it's afraid would happen if it didn't make you anxious around roads. Driving on them or crossing them with your sister.

HADDON: Ah, man. (This is said with compassion. I make a sound of enquiry to signal that I'm still there and listening.) He doesn't want anybody to get hurt.

EMMA: He wants to protect you from physical hurt, yes? (Haddon nods, then shakes his head at this realization.) Let him know that it makes sense, would you?

HADDON: Uh huh, and he doesn't want me hurting anyone else either.

EMMA: Does that make sense too?

HADDON: Sure does.

EMMA: And Haddon, see if he likes doing what he's doing, making you feel anxious, so you take extra care or avoid certain things.

HADDON: No, no he doesn't. He knows I'm a good driver really, or I am when he doesn't make me anxious ... He's tired. (Protectors are often tired and feel burdened by the responsibility they carry, such as keeping this young man and other road users safe.)

EMMA: Haddon, this might seem a strange question, just go with it if you can. Ask if this part protects anyone on the inside. It might be that someone is already burdened with hurt from driving a car or ... ?

I'm curious about the exile being protected who may need attention and even unburdening, which in turn could bring greater relief to this protector.

HADDON: Yes, he says, yes. (Haddon looks up at me for the first time in a long while, and I smile encouragingly. Then, responding to his look of worry, I remind us both.)

EMMA: Let's remember, there's no rush. (I'm aware the end of the session is approaching.) Do you still sense this protective part? (He nods, head back down and hands clasped.) Check with him how it is to be in connection with you like this.

HADDON: Good, it's good.

EMMA: That's great, and I'm wondering if we can start drawing to a close now. So, ask this part if there's anything else he wants to share with you briefly for today. (Haddon shakes his head.) Okay, if it feels appropriate, ask this part if there's anything he needs from you between now and when we next meet.

HADDON: He wants me to restrict driving lessons to the car park for now.

EMMA: Sure, that makes sense. How is that for you?

HADDON: Yeah, yeah. I'll do that. (Haddon raises his head and is swiftly back in the room in the present.)

EMMA: Well done, Haddon. Have you any questions or comments you'd like to share? (He shakes his head) No, then maybe you could keep a look out for this part, and we'll follow up together next time.

HADDON: Sure.

Welcoming Haddon's exile

Over the next couple of sessions, I follow up with Haddon as this issue remains live:

EMMA: Hello, Haddon, how are you and how have things been since we last met?

HADDON: Good. Yeah, my driving lesson went fine. Mr Marshall talked about driving on the road again.

EMMA: He did? How was that for you?

HADDON: Well, sure, I know I've got to do it sometime, parts of me want to, that's the point after all. But I felt that part again, in my chest and I remembered I'd promised, you know.

EMMA: I do know, yes. So, this part, the one with the anxiety signalled 'Hi' so you'd notice him, yes? (Haddon nods.) And how did you respond?

HADDON: I put my hand on my chest and breathed is all, but I thought in my head, 'I get it, I won't do it until you're ready.' That felt good, like something opened up inside.

Haddon is befriending this part in real life; he is aware of it and in turn, the part is aware of the Haddon-who's-not-a-part.

> EMMA: Great, that's great, it sounds like this part is trusting you? (He nods.) Would you like to meet with this part now, here in therapy?
> HADDON: Sure. (He rubs his hand against his chest automatically.)
> EMMA: How are you feeling towards this part as you notice it?
> HADDON: I'm feeling kind of chill (I sense I can take that as Haddon-speak for calm) and I'm kind of curious to know what the problem is with driving on the road.
> EMMA (gently): That sounds wise. Ask this part. (I can see he's a little more emotional than usual, and want to make it clear I'm still with him.)
> HADDON: He tells me he doesn't want me on the road in case I get road rage and hurt someone ... and because cats get killed on the road. (Ah: this feels important. Emotion is surfacing for Haddon, so I check out that's okay for his system.)
> EMMA: There's something about cats. But before we go there, can I ask you to check inside that it's okay for you to proceed to any strong emotions inside about this?

With access to my own Self-energy and leaning into the holding that IFS provides, I want to indicate to Haddon and any concerned parts that I am able and willing to accompany Haddon as he goes towards – not away from – emotion. And we want to get permission from the system if we can:

> HADDON (closing his eyes): Uh huh, everyone's okay with that. (He takes a deep breath, and there's moisture around his eyes.) My cat got run over right around when my little sister was born; we've never had a cat since. Miggs she was called. I couldn't cry or get upset, had to shut all that down and be happy for Mum and her new man, concentrate on the new school.
> EMMA: Ah, that makes sense. As you recall all this, just check and see if there's a young part holding anything about this who needs you.
> HADDON: No, it feels kind of good to remember her. She was the best, you know; everyone loved her.

As he recalls losing the family cat, Haddon turns his head to brush his eyes against the tops of his arms. I'm sensing things could go either way, away from the grief or towards it. My intuition tells me to persist, that his system wants to move towards it, not away:

> EMMA: As you remember the loss of your cat, Haddon, is there a part who couldn't cry that needs you?' (He's nodding and seems choked up.) Are you okay to feel what you're feeling? It's not overwhelming you?
>
> HADDON: Uh huh, s'fine ... I can sense a younger version of me, so alone, alone with a lot.
>
> EMMA: Absolutely. And how are you feeling towards this younger version of you?
>
> HADDON: Yeah, curious. I'm glad I know they're there; I want to be here for them now.
>
> EMMA: That's great. It's not too late to go back and be there for that young part of you.

Over the next couple of therapy sessions, Haddon witnesses this part's grief, anger and confusion – all of which are normal human emotions, but which can be so often unwelcome and exiled from experience.

With my support, Haddon enquires about whether the part who is holding his grief wants his assistance. He discovers his young part wants to say a proper farewell to the family cat Miggs, and let the tears fall without anyone getting upset with him. Haddon's Self arranges a dignified funeral, and his young part weeps healing tears. Before joining Haddon in the here-and-now, his young part wants to get rid of the burdens he was carrying:

- *Big boys don't cry.*
- *Be strong and man up.*
- *Being a bother is bad.*

The little one asks Haddon to build a bonfire to burn up those beliefs, which he does; they blow away in the smoke. I invite Haddon to check with the part that it's released everything to do with his cat's death. The part confirms it has, and Haddon encourages him to invite whatever qualities he chooses to replace his burdens. He chooses courage and playfulness. And then, cheerful and brave, he comes to be with Haddon in the present, in a cosy nook in his chest.

Now that Haddon's young exile has been healed, we return to the part who was fearful about driving on the roads. Haddon makes sure this protector is aware of what's happened on the inside – it is – and asks if it still has concerns. The part seems duly impressed and calmer, no longer afraid that Haddon will be overwhelmed by his young part's hidden grief. Courageously, this protector gives Haddon its consent to proceed with driving lessons on the road, and asks to check in regularly. Haddon readily agrees and sends his appreciation to everyone inside.

Welcoming your exiles

Unlike Haddon, you may not have an IFS therapist to turn to. So, what might you do if one of your exiles makes its presence known by sharing strong feelings with you?

Firstly, stay steady. Your protectors are likely to be very concerned that the exile's pain will overwhelm you, which is precisely the outcome they are desperate to avoid. Knowing that concern, you can calmly ask any panicky or reactive protectors to relax back so that the you-who's-not-a-part can be with the exile to help it feel a connection with Self – not for long, just momentarily, no more. If the protectors allow such a brief connection to be made, great; if not, take their no for an answer – just send an inner message to the exiled part to say that your Self knows it is there and will keep it in mind going forward. Even a tiny promise like that can help the system immensely.

If your protectors will allow you a bit of contact, see if the exile, with your help, can keep the you-who's-not-a-part in mind and feel a gentle, persistent connection with you. Exiles sometimes like to have or hold golden threads linking them to our hearts; some like to have a teddy bear to hold or a blanket to soothe them. Sometimes exiles spontaneously relocate inside, somewhere closer to the present or more central physically (the heart can be a favourite place for exiles). Naturally, check with protectors that any such changes feel safe enough for them not to double down in their efforts of keeping the exiles locked away. To just the extent that your system allows, gently and regularly hold the exile in mind.

If your protectors simply refuse to allow you *any* contact with an exiled part who's in pain, or if the exile overwhelms your protective system with emotions that get in the way of daily life, you might consider securing some IFS therapy to meet your exile and take them through the IFS steps of healing with support. **Appendix 3** may offer you some guidance here.

Releasing phobic reactions

A mild fear, like Haddon's nervousness about driving, can be distressing enough. Intense and overwhelming fears, called phobias, can place a heavy emotional toll on a person's system and block a significant amount of Self-energy from being freely available inside. There is no reason to feel shame at having phobias: they are strong protective strategies that combine protector activity and exile memory. Releasing phobias sooner rather than later may build trust in the system between parts and Self and free up some confidence. Certainly, my confidence and sense of efficacy increased noticeably as I shed various phobic reactions and the patterns of avoidance that went with them. Here I share IFS Senior Trainer Mike Elkin's phobia protocol, including a fictionalized case example featuring Ingrid and her fears of snakes.

Mike describes a phobic reaction as what happens when a regular level of anxiety like Haddon's goes through an amplifier and feels intolerable to the person experiencing it. (If Haddon hadn't addressed his protector's fear of driving by healing the exile who motivated it, it might well have evolved into a phobia over the years.) The person suffering that amplified emotional response will go to all sorts of lengths to avoid those feelings, avoiding whatever activates the phobic reaction. The level of amplification defines the phobia, not the level of danger presented by the trigger. In the UK, for example, spiders rarely pose an actual threat to life and limb, but many people have extreme, or phobic, reactions to them.

Although Mike is a trained hypnotherapist, he reassures us such training and skills are not strictly necessary to work with phobias using IFS. It is possible to follow the steps below to achieve good results for yourself. In fact, someone overcame a phobic reaction of their own when reading the pre-edited draft of this book!

Using these steps may significantly reduce the emotional charge in your system, *but* it's important to remember that your parts do not have to change their behaviour as a result. It is possible that some parts will want to change behaviour and 'test out' the success of the phobia resolution. But go cautiously, and allow any changes to embed themselves for a while. If you have released a fear of heights, for example, you will want to make sure *all* of your parts consent before you book a trip to London to go up the Shard, or to New York to ascend the Empire State Building to take in the view.

If you decide to work with a phobia of your own, now might be a good time to consider how you will manage the process and make a record. Will you record the steps for yourself? Will you ask a friend to read them out to you and be there with their Self-energy to amplify yours? Maybe you will have someone you trust on standby to lend support should you need it.

Mike Elkin's phobia protocol

1 **Contact the part with the phobic reaction and ask it to unblend.** Place your attention on the phobic feeling without

letting it become strong; a mere hint is sufficient. With your attention on the feeling, notice the part holding that feeling and ask it both to communicate with you *and* to separate from you. Ask the part to pull in its feelings a little, move back, or in some way provide a bit of distance. The point is to have enough access to Self-energy that you are not overwhelmed by the phobic reaction and can pay close attention.

2 **Access your Self-energy.** You know what to do next: ask yourself, 'How do I feel towards this part with the phobic reaction?' Notice your answer and any reactions towards the part. Any reactions to the part that are not friendly curiosity can be asked to unblend and give space. (They can watch if they wish, but from a distance.) As always, take 'no' for an answer: if protective parts refuse to consent to this process, back off and try again another time.

3 **Ask the part for a memory.** Once you have inner consent to approach the part holding the phobia, ask that part to focus on the phobic sensations and let a related memory from childhood come into its awareness and have it share that recollection with you when it arises. The part does not need to let the memory overwhelm it; just a bit of the memory is enough.

4 **Scan the memory for a shameful feeling.** In that memory will appear a younger version of you, a child. This may be a little one you know, or an exile you're meeting for the first time. As you turn your loving curiosity towards the child, have the part who is holding the phobic reaction stay nearby and watch your inter-action. This isn't the time to go into the whole memory in detail. Rather, get curious about any emotions that the child is feeling, but believes to be unacceptable. Mike tells us that the child in the memory 'thinks that the fact he or she is having this feeling means that there is something seriously wrong with his or her character'. So, notice the combination of the feelings *and* the self-judgement about having them. The child's feelings will certainly be understandable to the you-who's-not-a-part as you listen.

5 **From your Self-energy, reorient or update the child in the memory.** From a place of open-hearted acceptance, clarity and confidence, help the child in the memory understand that there is nothing wrong with them or their feelings. Persist and stay

present, be playful if that helps, until the child in the memory really grasps that they did nothing wrong. Their feelings made sense then and make sense now. Notice how the child in the memory feels after discovering this; there will usually be a sense of relief and release. When it feels right, let the child in the memory know that you are returning to the part burdened by the phobic reaction. If it feels right and possible, and the child wants it, tell the child part in the memory you will return to them another time.

6 **Turn back to the part with the phobic reaction.** Still accessing your Self-energy, ask the part to bring to mind the trigger for their specific phobic reaction, whatever it is. At this point, there should be *no* phobic response. If some extreme fear persists, ask the part to imagine other aspects of the phobic experience to discover related memories and interact with those as before.

Ingrid uses the protocol to work with her phobia of snakes

To help bring Mike's protocol to life, I'll tell you a story about an imaginary client named Ingrid, married and a mum of two, who has a phobia of snakes. She had researched the recommended treatment methods people with phobias are advised to undergo, but cognitive behavioural therapy (CBT), exposure therapy, hypnotherapy and taking anxiety medication held no appeal for her. Even emotional freedom technique (EFT) seemed 'too much', as it involved focusing on the distressing or disturbing feelings, which Ingrid's system was desperate to avoid.

Ingrid lives in a part of the world where she is unlikely ever to come across a snake accidentally, so ignoring the phobia altogether was a perfectly reasonable solution. But now she and the family have booked to go on a holiday of a lifetime – to a place that has snakes. Ingrid wants IFS sessions to focus on this, and we arrange to meet online.

I guide Ingrid to focus lightly on the disturbance that arises when she brings a snake to mind:

EMMA: Just lightly, you're not inviting the part to flood you with its distress. You're inviting the part carrying that distress to make itself known to you.

INGRID (closing her eyes): Okay, yes, I sense a young part with a horrible writhing sensation in its belly, in my belly.

EMMA: That's it, now ask the part to help us. See if it is willing to pull that sensation into itself and then give you space both from itself and the sensation. (Ingrid nods – vaguely at first – and then with commitment.)

INGRID (points to a window seat in the room where she is): Okay, I sense the part has gone to sit over there.

EMMA: How do you feel towards the part you imagine over there in the window seat, Ingrid?

INGRID: Curious and glad it's here.

EMMA: Lovely. Now, see if the part can just lightly focus on that disturbing sensation associated with the phobia and let a memory come to them. Any memory, it doesn't have to make sense to the part.

INGRID: Mm, hmm.

EMMA: I'm guessing that's happened? (Ingrid nods.) Is there a child in that memory, Ingrid?

INGRID: Yes, she looks like a young version of me. My father's trying to teach me to swim and—

EMMA: There's no need to dwell on the memory for now. Can you be curious? (She nods.) Does the young version of yourself sense your curiosity? (She nods again.) Great, so get curious and check in with the child in the memory about the emotions and reactions she's having ... Does she think those feelings are unacceptable? ... Does she worry that they make *her* completely unacceptable?

INGRID: Wow. She's ... , I'm ... I mean emotions weren't welcome in my family.

EMMA: That makes sense, doesn't it? (Ingrid nods gently.) Show her you get that, and ask if there is more she can share about what was so unacceptable that makes her feel so badly about herself.

INGRID: She's confused and scared and feels very, very alone, even though she seems to be the focus of her father's attention. It's like he's not seeing her. He's not seeing her fear; she's frightened of the water, but he dismisses that because he's with her, like that was supposed to change everything.

EMMA: Is this okay for you, Ingrid?

INGRID: Yes, she can feel me with her. She's been trapped in that pool a long time with these big feelings. She thought she was just the worst daughter in the world for wanting it to end, wanting him to stop. She felt so out of control and didn't trust him to keep her safe.

EMMA: You're both doing great, Ingrid. Tell her you're getting this. (She nods and is holding herself with arms crossed across her body). Let her know that all her feelings make sense and are valid; she doesn't need to feel bad about these strong reactions. Let her know that what she's feeling is normal.

INGRID (nodding, shedding some gentle tears): She's feeling relieved, she's jumped into my arms and is going to stay with me now.

Notice what just happened: even without going through the healing steps described in the last chapter, this young part of Ingrid has been retrieved spontaneously – taken out of that place and time in which she was frozen.

EMMA: Great, have her be with you. Is it okay with her if you check in with her regularly?

INGRID: She'd like that. We'll spend some time together later and I'll show her round – does that make sense?

EMMA: Absolutely. You've really connected, and she wants to be part of your life. You and she may do further IFS together, or this may be enough for now. Yes?

INGRID: That makes sense.

EMMA: But before you come fully back to the present, as it were, check with the part in the window seat, would you?

INGRID: It's feeling relief, too. It's focusing on its belly and there's nothing there, no squirming. (She laughs delightedly and I'm grinning broadly.)

EMMA: Brilliant. See if you'd both like to do an experiment for a moment. (Ingrid opens her eyes and nods to me.) Invite the part – if it's willing – to momentarily think of safely coming across a snake on your holiday and see what happens.

INGRID: Nothing! I wouldn't want to approach it; it might be poisonous. But there's no charge there, the awful feelings have gone. Is that right? Can that be possible?

EMMA: Yes, it really can be possible, and that swiftly. Hopefully now there will be more spaciousness inside your system and you might experience your embodiment differently, too. But no rushing off to buy a snake or go to the reptile house at the zoo!

I say this playfully, but it feels important. Ingrid's system doesn't have to prove itself to anyone, and neither does yours.

Attending to safety as a primary caregiver

Having chosen to read this book, you might have parts who want you to be the best you can be. What you've learned about IFS so far might already have made a difference; you may already feel less discomfort or distress, or feel more confident and empowered at times. Now you are more connected to your inner family, I encourage you to think of yourself as a parent to your parts – as the person who is responsible for creating and maintaining their feelings of safety. Just as you would with outer-world children, you intervene in your parts' conflicts, attend to their fears, and support them to coexist as best they can.

Here are some tips to help you (and your parts) adjust to your role as primary caregiver in your internal family:

- Parts cannot successfully change other parts, even if they want to; only Self brings such transformation.
- Parts don't have to like each other. Mutual respect and awareness of inner interconnection can be enough to ensure that everyone inside is 'on the same team'.
- Parts may be so focused on their job or role that they may not realize it's having a hurtful impact on another part inside, or on the physical body, or on external others. It's okay to explain consequences simply and gently without blame; if possible, negotiate for a compromise or reduction in the behaviours that lead to harmful effects.
- Remind protectors that they *all* have positive intentions for the system, even if their tactics are vastly different. (**Chapter 8**, on polarizations, will discuss tactical differences in depth.)

Like external children, of course, your parts will often refuse to behave in the ways you want them to. As we've seen, they have minds of their own – and their apparent waywardness is often down to perfectly reasonable fear. When you encounter internal intransigence, remember an IFS mantra: 'What's in the way, is the way.' Here are some ideas to bear in mind when your IFS journey isn't going as expected:

- Protectors block access to Self, but it's not malicious; for them, it's a must (until they understand otherwise). They have sound reasons.
- Don't expect parts to trust Self too much too soon. Don't ask them to trust you all at once: start by asking only, 'Let me be curious; let me be present.'
- Reassure your parts that no one will be punished for protecting you, or for having been locked away, or indeed for anything.
- Let parts know that you understand that they are doing the best with the hands that were dealt to them.
- Offer any relevant, tailored updates to parts who block your curiosity. If a part is concerned about 'doing IFS wrong' – this is common – update it about the nature of this enquiry: 'This isn't like homework; I'm not grading anyone. I'm just curious to get to know you.'
- Be alert for the presence of Self-like parts who want to manage things. Practise asking yourself, 'How do I feel towards … ?'
- With an open heart and genuine curiosity, ask inside if anyone has concerns about getting to know parts.
- If a part shows itself, acknowledge it and make a note while asking inside, 'Who has concerns about me meeting with this part?'
- Proceed to greet and meet the part that showed up unless another part was concerned, in which case that part might become the focus of attention for now.
- Whichever part is the focus part, if you already have some awareness of it and it of you, address its fears. Alternatively,

if it's a part you've not met before, you may want to befriend the part using the 6 Fs.

- Respond appropriately to any parts with opinions about setting aside regular time for attending inside.

For more tips about how to handle challenging internal moments, see Section 4 on troubleshooting.

Journal prompt

Checking in

- Are you aware of any fears that seem interesting to explore further? If so, what concerns arise when you consider exploring those fears?
- Are you enjoying your journey beneath your surface? What has surprised you so far?
- Is a part piling on pressure for a specific outcome or destination? If so, be curious.

7

Self-leadership techniques

In this chapter, I provide practical ways for you to lead your system:

- The room technique
- Other helpful kinds of rooms
- Gathering round
- Embodying parts to unblend.

Some of these exercises may make sense early in your journey with IFS, some may not. See if you can bring curiosity and an approach of experimentation to all that I offer. Let any parts with 'shoulds', 'musts' or wanting to *get it right* take a back seat if they are willing. Perhaps invite them to speak to you first about their concerns (which you can address) so they can 'give you the floor', or at least enough space inside to be present for and with them.

The room technique

Our parts often make themselves known in response to external people in our lives – particularly those we find frustrating, alluring or otherwise activating. A popular IFS exercise, sometimes called the 'fire drill', is very helpful there. It helps us become aware of any part or parts that get activated or triggered in response to another person. Try it and see how you go. Give yourself permission to do what feels right for you. At the end of this section, to provide a real-life context, there is a case example of someone using the room technique and getting to know some protectors. Haddon also makes a reappearance.

I'll present a multisensory version of the exercise, but you might want to adapt it for your system. Disregard what *doesn't* fit for you and adapt as needed. (Some of us have parts who write in books using pencil, who underline or even highlight text; all are okay with me. However, you might want to check for concerns inside before committing to any such annotations!)

Setting the scene

First attend to comfort and set up your space so you can turn inward to do a You-turn. (You might turn your phone to Airplane mode, lie down, have pen and paper handy, set a timer in case you nod off, and so on.)

If it feels comfortable, become conscious of your breathing and of your body, inside and out. Ascertain if you feel curious and open enough to proceed. Ask any parts with concerns to come forward as you begin; address their concerns and negotiate with them. (Not all parts have to be present for all our activities inside.) A time to do this exercise is when your nervous system is in a relatively regulated state – when you feel calm, open to connection, and have access to your inner steering wheel. If that is your state now, ask inside for an example of someone who is *mildly* activating to a part or parts of you. (The 'mildly' is important if this is your first experience with this exercise. Don't start by dwelling on a lost love or a bitter enemy!)

Once you have that mildly activating person in your mind's eye, if it feels comfortable, imagine them in a special, closed room with a one-way mirror and a door that only opens from the outside. You and your parts are on the outside of the room, observing the person through the one-way mirror; the person cannot see you.

If your system isn't primarily visual, you can set up the room in another way. If you'd rather, you can imagine hearing the person speaking (while you and your parts are not heard), or recall your felt sense of what it is like to experience the person (while they cannot feel your presence). The point of the room is to establish a sense of containment and safe distance between that person and your system.

The person doing their thing and parts' reactions

Now you have this mildly activating person in awareness, imagine them doing, saying or being whatever it is that activates your parts. You and your parts can watch them, hear them or sense them doing their thing; they are in the room, unaware they are being observed. Because of the separation between you and the person, your parts won't become overwhelmed by their reactions to this person, the way they might in real life. Instead, the idea is to notice who inside becomes activated and how. Bringing some of the curiosity of a visiting anthropologist may be helpful here. What do you notice? Feelings may arise among your parts, or thoughts, or an impulse to move, do or say something.

If your parts' responses feel too many or too rapid, notice your breathing again, and ask parts not to overwhelm your consciousness but come forward one at a time to tell you how they're feeling about the person in the room.

Responding to parts' reactions

As you maintain hold of the inner steering wheel, acknowledge each part's reaction. 'Hello, annoyance in my fists,' you might say to yourself, out loud, or on paper if that's what you prefer. Focus attention on the part's reaction if it feels comfortable: 'I notice you.' Initial reactions that seem to come from nowhere may gradually flesh out into a separate part or parts. As you go, welcome what each part shares with you about how the person in the room activates them. Validate what each part shares; affirm that it makes sense for each part to react as it does.

Introducing distance

Once each activated part feels understood, ask all of them to step away from the room the person is in. For example, they might go behind you, so you are between them and the person in the room, or wear noise-cancelling headphones so they cannot hear the person. Others may imagine themselves in a bubble of light which prevents the person's energy from affecting them. Remember, in the inner realm, in the presence of Self, imagination can create and change reality in a way that is vastly different from in the outside world. The idea here is for your parts to let the you-who's-not-a-part, your Self, take responsibility for interacting with the activating person. Now that they've shared their feelings about the person, they are letting your Self take the lead in the interaction.

Noticing shifts

Notice if it feels any different inside now. How does it feel in your body, your breathing, and so forth? Ask your parts to notice that *you* are there to interact with the activating person. Next, with your parts maintaining their distance, have the person in the room again do, say or be whatever it is that activates your parts.

Ask yourself as this happens, 'How do I feel towards this person now?' Ideally, you can now access curiosity towards the person. You may even feel some warmth towards them – any of the qualities you associate with Self.

If one of your parts reacts at this point, acknowledge them and address any fears they may have around letting you be present, handling this situation, without their reactivity – just for now. See if they'll trust you to be present and in the driving seat in this exercise *and* the next time they encounter this person in real life. If some parts shame other parts for their reactivity – *There's no need to make a fuss*, or *Pull yourself together, you're embarrassing yourself* – gently but clearly remind everyone that *all* reactions make sense, and *no* part's reaction is shameful.

Going forward

Now that your parts have let your Self take responsibility for interacting with the mildly activating person, you can take your leave of the room and the person in it; that person can go back to wherever is right for them.

To bring an end to the exercise, withdraw with your parts to somewhere pleasant and negotiate to let *you* be present to interact with this person in the real world, just as they did in imagination. If some parts don't want to encounter the person at all in real life, they don't have to; all parts do not have to be present at all times. For example, my fun-loving parts do not tend to take part in typing book chapters, while my writing parts do not join in with other parts at party time. (As you **'sell' unblending** in this way, parts might notice they can reap benefits from conscious – that is, by choice and design – unblending or relinquishing the inner steering wheel.)

Lastly, please offer some appreciation inside for how parts step up to protect the system, and for participating in this exercise to whatever extent was possible. If it feels true for you, tell your parts you intend to come back to them at another time; you could even agree when and how. Or reassure them you will welcome them when they next become activated – if that seems likely.

> ### 'Selling' unblending to parts
> Protectors can fear unblending or leaving space for Self, even if they would much prefer not to be driving the psychic bus. From your inner confidence, clarity and creativity, speak to reassure them that unblending means they will feel less alone and overwhelmed. Allowing Self to be there for them signals that appreciation and validation are on the way. Asking them to give space is *not* about removing their control or getting rid of them. 'All parts are welcome' is meaningful only if the welcomer is available.

June and her parts encounter a troublesome neighbour

Setting the scene

To bring the room technique to life, I'll tell you the story of an imaginary client called June, who has come to IFS late in her therapy journey. She is beginning to warm to the idea of meeting her parts in sessions. An encounter with an older man in the neighbourhood has riled up some of her parts, which gives us an opportunity to access them using the room technique.

The person doing their thing and parts' reactions

I lead June in imagining the older guy in the imaginary room doing what he does in real life. I ask her how she feels towards him as she sees him there, and her parts start talking at once.

The first part shows up: *He pounces on passing women and then talks at them; it's like being pinned down with no way out.*

A second part reacts: *We try to talk with him in a civil way, but when we share our experiences, he trashes them. He dismisses what we have to say and deliberately misunderstands so he can just say what he's already said again!*

A third part joins in: *Yes, and the last time he was out there loitering like that, we didn't go within speaking distance; I made sure we stayed out of range.*

Responding to parts' reactions

I lead June in acknowledging these parts and appreciating them for showing up now. I ask her how she feels towards all three of them. She feels curious, welcoming and connected to them. I get a sense she is enjoying meeting with them, and they seem okay with being thought of as a trio or team. She tells them (and me) that she gets what they're saying and that their responses make sense. She's glad to hear from them now and wants to be there for them and their experiences in the future. I ask her to have the three parts notice her, how old she is, and how it feels for them to be in her curious and welcoming presence like this.

June reports back to me that the first one to have spoken feels some relief; the second is mollified at being listened to and taken seriously – *not patronized*, as it says. The last to share feels some pride in using avoidance tactics. They seem to enjoy noticing each other, too.

Introducing distance

At my suggestion, June invites all three parts to step behind her, and they agree. They watch as she turns back to the man in the imaginary room. I ask her how she feels towards *him* now. After enquiring, she says her heart now feels more open to him, and the parts behind her seem less affected, too. Part number one observes that the man reminds them of someone from their childhood who did not treat young June well. The part is pleased to be updated regarding the difference between the two men, and to know that this person is not a relative or friend, but a neighbour to whom June owes nothing beyond a polite nod of greeting.

Noticing shifts

I check how June is. She feels calmer, and the sense of camaraderie between the three parts continues; they are not alone in their discomfort. The first to speak, who felt some powerlessness, is pleased to notice the action taken by the part who took evasive action.

Interestingly, by the time June completes this room exercise, the part who had seemed the most angry (part number two) says aloud that maybe they don't need to take the man's behaviour so personally: *It says more about him than it does about us,* the part wisely suggests. (In case you are wondering, this happened without any coaching from me about being kind, giving the man the benefit of the doubt, or making allowances as he might be lonely, and so forth.)

Going forward

June still frequently walks past the house where this man lives with his wife, and it now seems that there was never really a problem. Parts feel confident that in the moment they can simply avoid him, or trust June to speak to the man for them.

Other helpful kinds of rooms

The 'fire drill' technique uses an imaginary room to help you and your parts manage relationships with external others. Here are two more rooms you can use inside: the first is the waiting room; the second I think of as a room of containment.

The waiting room

Let's say you have a part you're getting to know – for the sake of explanation, imagine the part of June who cleverly avoided the older man is a protective part of your system. You have progressed through the first three Fs – **find, focus, flesh out.** Then you check inside how you **feel** towards the part, looking for the characteristics of Self-energy. In this case, the answer to that question might be 'embarrassed' – which means that another part of you is embarrassed by the first one. You'd ask curiously, 'Ah, who's embarrassed?' Whereupon another part might come in, saying, *It's rude to avoid that elderly neighbour, he's probably lonely. You're so self-centred!*

Based on what you've learned of IFS so far, the thing to do now is to turn to the part who feels embarrassed by the one you were getting to know and explore its feelings. But your new ability to create imaginary rooms inside gives you another option: you can ask the embarrassed part, along with any other part that reacts, to go into a waiting room – somewhere comfortable and pleasant, where they won't have to witness your Self interacting with the part you were getting to know. That way, these parts can allow your enquiry to proceed without hovering, ready to lodge objections.

Explicitly appreciate each part for agreeing to go into the waiting room. If many parts are having reactions, you could even broadcast a system-wide invitation: 'All parts who are uncertain about me getting to know this part, I'd appreciate it if you were to hang out somewhere nice – on your own or together – for just a few minutes, until we've finished. You don't have to watch or listen if you would rather not.' (Giving a time limit can help parts be willing to cooperate.) You then return to getting acquainted with the initial part.

If parts of you think the waiting-room technique seems a bit rude or controlling, maybe this will help: think of it as creating quality time for you and just one part to be together, just as an external parent might in the outside world. If you have more than one child, you don't always want one of them interrupting when you are trying to spend quality time with another. Having said that, of course, if the interrupting child is expressing genuine fear, need or urgency, then it would be appropriate to divert attention to them until their situation is settled. (Or until their perception of the situation as urgent has become more realistic, if that's appropriate.) Then you, as the parent, can return to the initial one-to-one conversation.

The room of safe containment

It's not just people on the outside who activate parts in us. Parts on the inside sometimes upset, frighten or even terrorize other parts. We can create secure rooms for working with such parts to preserve the whole system's safety.

Say you want to befriend a part of a sort most of us have inside, a harsh inner critic, who protects us by shaming or bullying other parts of the inner family. The parts who get shamed and bullied might understandably object to letting you get to know the critic! In that case, it can help to build a secure chamber in your inner world, where you and the critic can talk in private, so other parts won't have to hear or see your interactions. If the critic agrees to join you there, other parts can relax. Alternatively, parts who are afraid of the critic can be provided with their own secure room, where they can be safe and snug while the two of you interact.

Paying attention to safety is important in every family, inner and outer. For example, parents in the outside world know it's important not to have certain grown-up conversations or do certain activities with their children around. In the same way, our inner team members, who are often young and relatively defenceless, sometimes need our intervention to shield and protect them from others on the inside. Safe rooms can help.

Haddon and his critical part

You remember Haddon from the last chapter, the young man learning to drive? In our IFS sessions together, Haddon and I become aware that there is a part of him who criticizes Haddon when he's behind the wheel during his driving lessons.

Initially, the driving instructor intervened when he noticed Haddon verbally beating himself up for making a mistake, sometimes even hitting the steering wheel with the heel of his hand. 'This beating yourself up isn't going to work,' the instructor scolded. 'It's not worked for any of the people I've taught to drive, and you're not going to be the first.' But that only made the critical part come down harder on Haddon's mistakes.

Haddon and I invited the inner critic to be our focus for a few sessions. We invited parts who were afraid of the critical energy of this part to sit tight in a safe room while we worked with it, which they readily agreed to do. Once the fearful parts were secure elsewhere inside, Haddon was able to spend time with the critical one, who could sense Haddon's spacious, grounded, calm and calming presence. At my prompting, Haddon suggested to this part that driving (whether during lessons in the car park or in future on the road) when feeling calm and spacious in this way was an ideal state to be in, rather than in an agitated or self-critical frame of mind.

The critic acknowledged the wisdom of that; since its ultimate aim was to protect Haddon from shame, it was willing to experiment with letting Haddon's Self take the lead during driving without its critical input. Together Haddon and the part negotiated a version of a 'waiting room': while Haddon drove in the front seat, the critic would view proceedings from the backseat, and debrief with Haddon *after* his lesson to review any mistakes.

Gathering round

Inner rooms can help our parts stay safely separate, but they can also bring our parts together. A simple and effective technique is to hold a gathering of parts in an inner space you create for that purpose. You might set up a meeting-room or a kitchen where everyone has space around the table, or you might build a camp-fire in the woods for everyone to gather round – anywhere of your choosing that parts agree to. If your system has much internal activation or conflict, you can bring parts together 'virtually', on an imaginary Zoom or Teams meeting or conference call. In this way, each part can feel it has its own space and can leave as it wishes. Get creative and curious about what would work best for your system.

Calling inner meetings is particularly helpful in decision-making or planning, when it's important to build internal con-sensus about external decisions that will affect the system as a whole. It can also be useful in a moment when your system is feeling unsettled or is dealing with a specific issue like ill health or an interpersonal problem. In such meetings, as in IFS gener-ally, all parts are always welcome. To help Self facilitate, it makes sense to have some tools at hand to help parts talk and listen to each other with respect and curiosity.

Integrating IFS with other decision-making practices

Gathering your parts round a table or campfire to make important decisions can help you use other decision-making techniques more skilfully. It's likely that you already have ways to make decisions, and I suggest you continue using them – but now in cooperation with all your parts. If you're in the habit of making pro–con lists, for example, you might bring your parts into the process like so:

- Introduce yourself and your present-day resources, and update the parts contributing to the process that you are responsible for including their responses in weighing up the situation, gathering more information if needed, and over time coming to a decision.

- Have any parts urgently trying to arrive at a decision relax back rather than taking over.
- Think of the lists of pros and cons as the desires, suggestions and wisdom of your parts. Invite them all to contribute to the list.
- As they do, remain curious and open to all that is being shared – don't side with a particular viewpoint, and don't let anyone veto other parts' contributions.
- If any parts start getting into conflict with each other, invite them to return their focus to the you-who's-not-a-part.
- Listen to and address parts' fears from a Self-led place.

Internal meetings with crayons

Ruth Culver, a certified IFS Level 3 trained practitioner, special-izes in offering IFS using guided intuitive drawing, which can be of great help in holding internal meetings.[1] She explains how she uses the practice for her own system:

> The train was running late, and I was travelling to facilitate a new workshop, in a new place, so I had a few unsettled parts. I automatically turn to paper and crayons when activated these days, so fished them out of my backpack. I drew a large oval to establish a conference table, adapting this IFS favourite for bringing multiple parts together to get a hearing. It's a handy process when time is short, taking as little as 10 minutes; though it can equally well fill a whole 60- or 90-minute therapy session, listening to all parts, going more deeply with some, and exploring many inter-relationships in the system. The brief version was all I needed on the train: I connected with each part in turn, noticing how it was feeling in or around my body, inviting it to pick a colour for itself and 'Take a seat around the table'. Before moving to the next part, I jotted down a few words the part was saying about its feelings and purpose – a witnessing process that helps parts feel heard, as well as helping me

stay connected and in flow with my system without needing to remember things. Once it seemed all the parts were
there around the table, evidenced by my activated feelings
relaxing into curiosity, I returned to re-connect to each part
in turn, asking them about their concerns and then about
their needs for the day. (Culver, 2023, pp. 226–8)

Ruth tells us that as she sat back in a calmer state, digesting what
she'd learned from her parts, she became aware of another pas-
senger, a young man named Lex:

Smiling, I asked if it was odd to see a grown woman using
kids' crayons on a train. He grinned back and asked what
I was doing. After hearing a little, to my surprise he asked
if he could have a go, because 'I'm doing my nut about a
big decision.' It emerged that he had been an under-17s
swimming champion, was on his way to a big competition,
and on the verge of giving up because he'd performed consistently badly since moving into the adult age group. He
asked me for instructions, so I checked inside briefly with
my concerned parts. They relaxed when I reviewed my sense
of Lex's Self-energy, and reminded them that being on a
train, and the business of drawing, would support us to simply gather information from parts, enabling them to enjoy
the relief of being heard and understood, without going to
the deeper places of the healing steps.
    One of my great passions for developing this method is
that a simplified version can be used without a therapist,
so I let Lex know that I was happy to guide him through
the mechanics, and I would listen, but wouldn't do any
therapy, nor give advice or interpretations. He agreed, and
I began simply by asking him to imagine that all the different opinions that were arguing in his head were coming in
one by one, like people arriving and taking a place at a table
together. For appropriate depth and pacing, I didn't ask him
to close his eyes or notice feelings in his body, just to 'focus
on one at a time then let that energy show how it's feeling
by making abstract marks with whatever colour feels right'.
    Lex took to it like a duck to water, scribbling violently
with a black crayon for the part furious about having no
social life, placing strong red parallel lines for the part saying

he should 'Stop complaining and get on with it', a rising orange spiral for one who was fed up with getting up at 4 AM on winter mornings to train, and slowing to create a soft pink haze for one who felt guilty about what his parents had sacrificed. The table quickly filled up with a dozen different parts, all with a few words written next to them, ending with a bright green swirl for the one who just loves swimming. He sat back and sighed, saying 'Wow, that feels better. It's like the chaos has chilled out.' A pause followed, and 'No wonder I've not been sleeping.'

Ruth writes that she looked Lex up on social media a few days later and saw a photo he'd posted of himself 'grinning and holding a trophy'.

Embodying parts: blending to unblend

Ruth tells that story in a chapter called 'Embodied unblending'. Both the inner meeting she called for her system and Lex's part-by-part drawing show what I call 'blending to unblend': inviting our parts to take up *more* of our consciousness as a way to make space for Self. We invite our parts to blend when they speak in our inner meeting rooms or express themselves through drawing, and as they do they open up more space for Self and for each other. We can all find creative ways to do this. Paradoxical though it may seem, inviting a part to blend safely so as not to overwhelm the system can feel freeing and therapeutic. Allow yourself to experiment: invite a part to amp it up, dance, sing, deliver a monologue or in some way more fully inhabit or be your body. In time, the part will either give way for another part to blend or for Self to come alongside and be with it, too.

Music and dance

Music and dance can be powerful ways to help parts 'blend to unblend'. Nic Wildes, a white queer transmasculine mental health counsellor in the USA, has written about their journey with IFS and gender. Over eight years or so, their system has become much more open, with willingness for soft and tender parts to be known inside and shared with others outside. At first, music was Nic's go-to means of connecting inside:

> For a long time, and likely because of [a] high degree of protection, it seemed that the easiest way for me to connect inside to my parts was through listening to music while walking and moving my body. Free from fear of external judgment and the belief that there is a 'right way' to connect internally, my parts seemed to have greater ease communicating with me through song lyrics. Over the years several have stood out as anthems and theme songs while others communicate Self's clear and tender response. (Wildes, 2023, p. 142)

Someone else I know prefers dancing to music when parts need attention. If a part experiences frustration with their intimate partner, they put music on when alone in the house and invite the part to move spontaneously to the music of their choice, making sounds, gestures and animating the body. At some point, there is enough space inside for Self to come alongside, acknowledging and gently validating the part: 'I get that you are angry about this; you and your anger are welcome.'

Playfulness and role-playing

Therapeutic theatre, psychodrama and dramatherapy can also help parts blend to unblend. A while back before I came across IFS, I attended a one-day introduction to a form of improvisational dramatherapy called developmental transformations (DvT), presented by the founder of the approach, David Read Johnson.[2] He asked for a volunteer to demonstrate a one-to-one session in which he and the volunteer client would enter a mutually created 'playspace' where they would embody, enact, and play with whatever was emerging for the client in the playspace. My hand shot up (do you have parts who do that, too?). Looking back on the session from an IFS perspective, I see that some of my parts blended just enough for David and I to notice and enjoy them, and in such a way that they could sense being noticed and enjoyed.

I started the session by going behind David (shy parts were present), while also trying to hold his hands. I ended up holding both of his thumbs, one in each hand behind his back. David then began walking, and I followed along doing a silly walk (embarrassed and playful parts were using my body). This got some laughs from the other students (that felt so good to some parts). Then it dawned on me that it was as if David was my 'prisoner' and I was his arresting officer (I like watching police procedurals). Still walking, we reached the side wall of the room. As I continued holding his arms behind him, he took more of an active hold of my hands then pushed himself forcefully against the wall while I remained in contact with him. Spontaneously, from inside of me, a shocked giggle escaped. David righted himself and did it again (a few times actually). David was play-acting being slammed against the wall by an imaginary arresting officer, me, using brute force!

Correctly, he had sensed that I might have an unknown urge (held by at least one part, if not more) to have power over him and slam him against the wall at will. In this playful, distancing and imaginary method, my part was invited to embody that impulse just a little, play with and enjoy it. How healing is that!

Journal prompt

Using inner rooms

If you tried any of the room techniques, what was that like for you and your parts? You might reflect on the kinds of rooms you created for your parts, and even invite them to let you know when using a room might be beneficial in the future.

8

Using IFS in everyday life

IFS isn't just for therapy: it's a practical way of living. Although I am a trained IFS therapist and this book contains some clinical case examples, my intention is to highlight the practical usefulness of using IFS to interact with your inner world from day to day. Our parts exist within us even when we are not in a therapy session, or even in therapy at all, but always: when we are at work, in the bath, hanging out with the kids, taking the dog for a walk and so forth. Parts inhabit our lives and our relationships even if we're not currently experiencing an emotional or psychological problem; Self is equally omnipresent, and available any time our parts agree to let it lead. I've written this book to assist in getting the word out onto the high street about inner multiplicity and Self.

Thus far I have focused your attention on thinking about yourself in terms of parts, being curious towards them, and having parts unblend and be available for a relationship with the you-who's-not-a-part – all in a deliberate and intentional way. Now I want to turn your attention to the many ways your Self and your parts interact from moment to moment as you move through the world together. As you probably know from daily life, nurturing effective and enjoyable relationships involves mastering the multifarious art of communication. In this chapter I offer various ideas about how to communicate with your system and the systems of other people.

Self-talk in the first-person plural

You may have encountered the idea of 'self-talk' from therapy or social media. IFS lets us interpret our 'self-talk' in an exceptionally nuanced way – not just as an inner clamour, but as an ongoing conversation among our parts. My self-talk has changed drastically over the years as I have become more attuned to my inner world, a change I notice when I think about how I respond to my occasional clumsiness. As I move around the world, I regularly bruise my legs and bash my feet. In the past, an inner voice would loudly cast blame: *Idiot!* The underlying message was strong: *Why are you bouncing off the furniture like this? What's wrong with you?*

These days, my responses are more varied and compassionate:

- I hold or rub the hurt body part.
- I let my parts say *Ouch!* out loud shamelessly, acknowledging the hurt.
- There's an internal recognition that no one's done anything wrong; accidents happen.
- And I feel a sincere compassion: *Oh dear, so sorry we've hurt ourselves.*

I'm not entirely sure who is speaking or responding in these recent ways, and I don't feel the need to analyse the interactions: it could be Self speaking, or it could be a part or group of parts. What I do know is that my system is benefiting from increased kindness and reduced self-blame. There is a great comfort in experiencing yourself not as a clumsy 'I' but as a compassionate 'we'.

Ash Chudgar (March, 2024), a fellow IFS enthusiast and communication expert, suggests that using the first-person plural pronoun 'we' can be healing all by itself:

> This is a handy trick to practice any time you're feeling *beside yourself* – undecided, torn, conflicted, irrational, or crazy. Such common human states of mind are much less unpleasant from a first-person plural point of view, believe it or not. Try it and see! This doesn't require any outward action, or even any particular effort of imagination. Just

saying the words in your head will do the trick nicely. For example:

- When an inner critic whispers, 'Ugh, you're disgusting,' take a breath before you react. Imagine that critical voice is a *part* of you – not all of you, for sure, but *somebody* inside you, with a perspective that should count. And together, you and this part of you constitute an *us*. So, you can say, in your head: '*We* are feeling disgusted at the moment.' And just like that, the critical part of you knows they're not alone: they're part of the *we* that you brought them into just by saying those words in your head. Magic!
- When a frightened inner child throws a tantrum in your belly, don't kick it out of consciousness for being such a stupid baby. Instead, include that inner child's experience: say, 'We're a little bit frightened right now.' And just like that, the little one inside of you has you for company, so things don't feel so scary.

Including various parts of yourself in the *we* of your inner dialogue is magic. But again, don't take my word for it – try plural pronouns out for yourselves.

'Ouch, we bruised my leg again!' feels very good to me.

How parts use the body to communicate

Depending on how your IFS journey and explorations with this book are proceeding, you may already have some open communication with some of your parts. That's great if so, and I'm pleased for you. And if that is not part of your current experience, try not to be disheartened: it's okay, truly. Here's something that might make sense to you: sometimes my body communicates *for* my parts. I'm not alone in this. Many people have parts who communicate *only* somatically, not thorough mental images, internal voices or even thoughts. Others of us experience a mix of inner communication styles. While our parts' embodied messages can be tricky to recognize at first, communication they are – and you can learn to respond skilfully.

Generally, I don't tend to suffer with headaches; they are very noticeable when they happen. I clearly remember a time (before IFS) when I attended a spiritual ceremony which fell outside of the Anglican religion in which I was raised. I knew some of the people attending the ceremony and had enjoyed meditating with them for some time. I wasn't aware of being nervous. However, as soon as we assembled for the ceremony, I became crippled by a headache so intense I needed to leave. Looking back now, it makes sense that someone inside, very uncomfortable with a non-Anglican ritual, was using my body to say a firm *No!* Or, as we jokingly say in my house, 'putting their foot down with a firm hand'. Unaware of multiplicity at the time, I had not communicated with parts about my intentions, nor enquired about their spiritual loyalties. I like to think I know a little better now, and my parts are still welcome to speak to my Self through my body.

Clara's laryngitis

IFS professionals have many colourful stories about how clients' parts communicate somatically, sometimes through **illness**. In our podcast for IFS professionals, my co-host Gayle Williamson shared the story of a long-term client I'll call Clara.[1] One of Clara's main protectors agreed to hand over her responsibilities to Clara's Self, but then immediately became concerned. The very next day, Clara lost her voice in a bad case of laryngitis. Gayle didn't think this could be a coincidence, and Clara agreed, recalling that her voice had gone at other significant points in her life.

With Gayle's support, Clara focused inside and found a part that was stopping her from expressing too much emotion or vulnerability. It shared that it silenced Clara to give her more time to work through things before responding to significant others in her life. Gayle led Clara to ask this silencing part about its present concerns. It explained it had picked up on the changes of greater openness and inner freedom within Clara, and believes it isn't safe for her to communicate with her family any longer. The part's positive intention was to silence Clara in order to keep her safe. The part also volunteered that it had been keeping Clara awake for several hours in the middle of the night to make her too tired to meet family obligations.

As the session ended, Gayle asked Clara to thank the part and negotiate with it a little. Clara told it that now she is aware it is there, and understands its concerns, it doesn't have to continue affecting her voice and keeping her awake in the night. She is listening. The client asks if the part would be willing to pull back over the next week, just to see how the Clara-who's-not-a-part handles her interactions with family. The part agreed to this. Clara reported to Gayle the next week that, the night of their last therapy session, she slept through to morning for the first time in a while; and on waking, her throat was just fine.

Illness and inner communication

Recognizing that a part may influence or use your body doesn't mean that *all* your bodily experiences can be reduced to your parts' efforts to communicate. Our bodies are incredibly complex, and our parts' activity may be *an* influence. When you experience physical symptoms, by all means check with your parts to see if they're involved – but consult a doctor, too!

Bringing curiosity to symptoms

Ruth Troughton, an IFS-trained mental health physiotherapist in New Zealand, gets curious about parts' contributions to the physical issues of her clients. When they work together, she asks questions to elicit understanding in the client regarding the role or purpose of a bodily posture, movement, sensation or somatic response, treating the physical symptom with the dignity Self offers all parts. She might ask:

- 'How does X response think it's helping you out?'
- 'I wonder why X body part feels it has to work so hard?'
- 'I'm curious why your brain/body feels it's not okay to let you go to sleep at night?'

Explicit curiosity can also elicit information regarding what Ruth calls 'implicit drivers' for patterns of movement, particularly any underlying fears: 'What does that body part think would happen if it didn't do what it does?' In her own words, Ruth writes:

> Questions about how long the part has been doing this role, as well as exploring perception of age are also enlightening, particularly regarding how empowered or how responsible the client feels. 'How old does this [leg/sensation] think you are?' In most cases the perception is that the person is significantly younger – usually under 10 years old, and sometimes more toddler or preschool age. Very occasionally the part believes the client to be older as was the case for one of my teenage clients, where the manager believed them to be at least 30, and where the client had very unrealistic expectations of themselves.
>
> I also sometimes ask what would need to happen for a part to stop feeling it needed to do its current task, and occasionally what alternate activity it would like to do instead. (Troughton, 2023, p. 57)

Ruth provides a couple of inspiring case studies, including one she calls 'Relieving the Night Watchman'. The client in this one is consistently unable to settle to sleep on her right side, though she can do so easily on her left side. They discover that the client has a protector, a gnome called Brian, who protects her by managing the transition from wake to sleep. This part has been active for ten years. Although this is initially a surprise to her, the client recognizes how it makes sense in the context of her experiences. It seems that Brian sees its role as protecting her from something coming from the left side, which it senses as weak, and is concerned that the client may also not be skilled at evaluating potential risk.

On one hand, Brian the gnome feels its role is threatened, as the client feels more empowered and has greater trust now in her own mind and judgement. On the other hand, he feels reassured to be updated about the client's new confidence. Brian especially appreciates being acknowledged and valued, and he agrees to observe the client's sleep rather than managing it. Next session, the client tells Ruth that, while falling asleep on the right side is still not as easy as on the left, she has noticed an improvement. She and Ruth continue working to address factors contributing to the strength and capacity of her left side.

How to interact with other people's parts

It is possible that one of the reasons you are reading this book is because you want to communicate more effectively with members of your external-world family. That makes sense: recognizing our own parts' activity is an excellent place to start. Once you recognize a part of you is activated at home, you can dialogue with it and negotiate with it to relax, so the you-who's-not-a-part can communicate with your external family member.

Being and communicating with a person in distress

Of course, that's easier said than done! Family members can activate our parts in ways no one else ever could, making them double down on their efforts to protect you. To explain how you can bring an IFS perspective to difficult interpersonal conversations, I want to talk about an especially activating one. One of the most challenging times to stay Self-led in communication is when another person is in distress, whether they are a child or an adult. Here are some ideas for how to respond rather than react.

Recognizing and responding to our own parts' activity is the place to start. Ideally, we want to be with a distressed other from a place of Self-energy and Self-leadership. Things usually proceed better when that is the case, and you may already have simple tools in your toolbox for how to not let a protective part of you leap into the driving seat in the moment. Some of them are quite simple:

- Mentally counting to ten
- Doing a breathing exercise or another pre-set behaviour
- Using a **mantra**.

Once you have a little access to Self, you can help your parts not take the other's distress personally. Remind them:

- The person's distress is coming from a *part* of them; it's not the *whole* of them.
- Just like them, other people's parts have positive intentions and that together with exiles they serve their system, doing the best they can with outdated knowledge and skills.
- Parts in distress are communicating and want that communication acknowledged and validated by the you-who's-not-a-part and if possible by their Self.

Using a mantra

It can be valuable to allow a short mantra to arise in and for your system for times when you need quick access to Self when parts are especially activated. My system's is 'I'm here. I'm here.' It comes with a release of breath and inner calming. When I am working with a client who's in distress, my mantra is: 'Let me be curious. Just let me be curious.'

To be with another person's distress in Self, we make it safe for our parts to unblend inside. Our parts need connection with Self, that loving, holding, alchemically curious energy. That can be particularly difficult for parents when their children are having a hard time. Anna Vincentz and Joel Bubbers offer a suggestion for such situations:

> This step is about being *with* the part that is triggered in relation to your child. You might not yet know what is going on inside of your child, you might only be aware of the reaction or behaviour of your child. Naturally, whatever is going on with your child is going to have an effect on you. Notice how you respond inside. Maybe you feel frustrated by their behaviour, or perhaps stuck and powerless. You might notice tightness or weakness in your body; you might have thoughts about your child: 'He is so spoiled!' or about yourself: 'I'm a horrible parent!' Whatever comes up inside of you is what you want to get to know, because this is coming from the part of you that is triggered.
>
> Get curious inward and see what else you notice about the part. Thoughts, words, feelings, sensations, images, memories ... then invite the part to notice you there as well. Let it know: 'I am here, I notice you' or expand the feeling in your open heart or inner light and invite the part to notice you there even a little.
>
> As in IFS therapy, the part noticing you and you being there with the part is the most important thing in this moment. It is the beginning of creating *secure inner attachment* whereby the part has someone to lean into (when there is enough trust) and no longer feels alone anymore to deal with everything.
>
> Once trust has been built, the part might have something it wants you to know and see. Like in Anna's example a part showed an image of almost drowning, trying to stay on the surface of a deep ocean. If you have time in the moment and feel you have enough inner foundation and Self-energy available at that point, invite it to share with you what it needs you to know. Oftentimes it's enough just having that inner connection and letting the part know you will return to it ...
>
> When it feels right, invite the part to find a safe space in or around your body or mind, to lean in a little and to give you some space. You might experience just a tiny shift (especially in the beginning of getting to know the part or if the part is coming on very strongly). That's okay too.
>
> Now it's time to focus outwards again. (2023, pp. 252–3)

145

Welcoming the other's distressed part from Self

Once you are resting in or coming from that open-hearted, centred, creative Self-led place of clarity, perspective and connectedness, you will be able to attune to and speak with a distressed child or adult. Here is an example of what I mean using parts language. Because you don't want to presume to understand someone else's inner system, you won't talk about 'parts' of the person; instead, you'll use your intuitions about their system to speak to imagined parts of them directly:

1 'I see how hard this is for you.'
2 'When a part of me is upset like this, it always makes sense somehow.'
3 'Would it be okay to tell me more about it?'

Referring to 'a part' of yourself can de-escalate the distress of the other's part. It highlights that there is more to their system than just them and their distress. In acknowledging a part in distress as a part, it can also reduce the fear of the distress held by other parts in the system.

Countering cultural messages about our parts

Sometimes in 'IFS-world', people make the mistake of thinking that being permanently 'in Self' is an achievable or desirable goal, and that being 'in a part' is a problem per se. I want to correct the record: being 'in a part' is normal. It's not extraordinary, it's how we do life; it's not shameful, it's fundamental to the human condition. This may be the first book you have come across that tells you: every part of every person has positive intentions and serves its inner family to the best of its ability.

Yet we are conditioned not to notice each other's parts and to ignore most of our own. Whenever we encounter our own internal multiplicity, culture gives us dire warnings that increase our fear of our own experience and have us do battle with or disown aspects of ourselves. Warnings like these:

- Think of the mind as a puppy; unless you train it, there's shit everywhere.
- Don't feed the monkey mind.
- Tame your inner gremlin.
- Which do you choose: the angel on one shoulder or the demon on the other?
- There are two wolves fighting within, the wolf of (a bad quality) and the wolf of (a good quality). The one you feed is the one that wins.
- Your mind is a dangerous neighbourhood. Don't go there alone.

Now that you know about IFS, you have an alternative: instead of battling against the complexity within ourselves, we can befriend and appreciate all parts of us, and our bodies. No one and nothing inside us deserves to be vilified. Inner conflict can feel so stressful and confusing, and be so time-consuming! It's no wonder that the advice about doing battle has an influence on us; it can give our parts the illusion of control in a world that really can't be controlled at all. Our managers in particular, tasked with preserving our social acceptability, are easily seduced by the cultural prejudices against internal complexity – particularly when they come into conflict with our firefighters!

Polarized pairs

Our managers' concerns about our other parts can be helpful trailheads for inner curiosity. Whenever you notice inner conflict, feel or sound harsh towards an aspect of yourself, or bounce between extremes of behaviour, remember that it is normal for parts to 'happen in patterns' – particularly between two parts whose strategies to care for us come into conflict. Do you recognize any of these opposing impulses from different parts of your system?

- work hard / rest and play
- diet and restrict / indulge
- put others' needs first / put my needs first
- seek approval / rebel
- stay in the relationship / leave the relationship
- keep the peace / speak up
- be strong / cling on
- stay safe / take risks
- be super helpful / be unavailable.

You may notice other tensions inside as well. In IFS, these common forms of inner conflict are called *polarizations*, and the parts on either side are said to be *polarized*. Before we explore how to approach such inner patterns, I want to emphasize certain things:

- A sequence or pattern of conflicting inner reactions is normal.
- Polarized parts have positive intentions and often even share the same goal.
- Such patterns are designed to bring or increase balance in the system, but often end up destabilizing it instead.
- Absorbed in conflict with each other, polarized parts block access to your inner leader, Self.
- Exiles are forgotten about as polarized parts do battle.

The first step in recognizing both sides of the pattern is simply to recognize the parts involved. This can be easier said than done, since it's common for just one side of the polarization to speak up.

Chloe appreciates Ann's hard worker

It's Chloe's birthday at the weekend, and her friend Ann is meeting with her for a quick coffee and cake. Chloe is excited:

she and her husband are taking a holiday to celebrate. But as usual, Ann is stressed about work, which dominates their conversation.

'I don't see how you can be so calm,' Ann says. 'I don't remember the last time my husband and I had a weekend away. I'm up to my neck in work, I've got my end-of-year tax return to calculate, Christmas to organize, and, as you will recall, he is useless. I don't think I'll be able to meet next month, I just can't see I'll have the time. But enough about me, we're meant to be celebrating your birthday. How's the cake?'

So, who do you think is driving Ann's inner psychic bus? A hard-working manager part is my guess – one who sounds extremely burdened, exhausted and worried about how it's going to manage all it has on its plate. You can probably sense how badly this hard worker needs befriending inside. This part might like to receive some inner appreciation for how hard it works and how well it serves the system. You can understand how unappreciated and alone it might feel – if it stopped to notice how it felt, which it may not have time to do.

As it happens, Chloe has read this book – so, in addition to being a bit annoyed, she senses that there's more to her friend than *just* that hard worker.

'Oh, Ann,' Chloe says, 'I hear how exhausted you're feeling, and unappreciated, too. But I wonder – is there another voice inside who tells you to stop putting in all the hours you do at work?'

This brings Ann up short, and she stops, silent for the first time in a while. Almost despite herself, she notices inside.

'Well, I guess yes, I'd love to be able to drop everything and go off on a break without a schedule to follow and no responsibilities.' She pauses; then her voice hardens. 'But that's just not possible.'

'I hear that,' Chloe replies kindly. 'It seems part of you is determined to work hard while another part wants the opposite, some freedom and escape to rest, perhaps.' Ann nods, thoughtful.

Polarization as a process

When only one side of an inner polarization speaks so strongly, at length and frequently, the opposing part is hidden in plain sight. Without the inner conflict around overworking, Ann's hard-working manager might have spoken once with pride about all it has going on and all it achieves, and that would have been that. As it was, the fact that Ann seemed so stuck was a great clue that pointed Chloe towards the unseen presence of a polarized part, who just wanted to go on holiday, too.

Like Chloe, you can take single-minded 'stuckness' as a clue about inner conflict. It begins with noticing when we speak with passion and at length from one voice, or are acting in a certain rigid way for a while. It's as though you've 'got the needle stuck' and the same tune is playing over and over. Once you notice that, you can ask a simple question inside: 'Is there anyone who believes the opposite or wants the opposite?'

When Chloe asked her friend a version of that question, Ann's hard-working part momentarily lost its tight grip on the inner driving wheel as someone else considered Chloe's question. But it quickly discarded the idea – 'it's just not possible' – because the hard worker honestly believes that *it is Ann*. Our managers are often 'Self-like' in this way: they believe they are alone inside, and that impulses that oppose their strategies are 'bad wolves' or 'demons' – malevolent, not quite real and to be defended against. But with just a little bit of access to Self, you can help a part of yourself who is 'stuck' in a hidden polarization unblend a bit, have a look around, and meet its inner opponent part to part.

Mediating between polarized parts

Depending on how heated the inner relationship is, you might want to be creative about how to facilitate an initial conversation between polarized parts. It often helps to provide some separation between them. Sometimes parts need to be in different rooms, as you've seen. But if it feels safe enough, you can achieve the necessary separation by bringing parts together in a shared but facilitated space.

Cece Sykes, one of the original IFS senior trainers, recommends having polarized parts sit either side of a table, with Self at the head.[2] Personally, I prefer to invite parts to sit across from each other in front of a fireplace (the kind in a drawing room in an old country house or large old-fashioned hotel) with me sitting in front of the fire and my parts facing each other in comfortable chairs on either side. There is a low table between the parts featuring a stately floral decoration, and a painting hangs imposingly over the fireplace. Set things up in your system in whatever way suits your parts and their tastes.

Once both parts are settled in, invite both parts to contemplate two key questions for protectors:

1 How are you trying to help (i.e., what is your positive intention for the system)?
2 What are you afraid would happen if you didn't do what you do?

Once Ann has learned a bit about her own system, she might bring her inner hard worker together with a comfort-seeking firefighter, who wants nothing more than to watch *Doctor Who* all day long – and, to the hard worker's horror, occasionally succeeds in making Ann do just that.

Ann's hard-working part might respond, *How am I trying to help? I want Ann to be successful and independent, loved and respected by her mother. And if I let up, this good-for-nothing layabout would take over permanently. You know how Ann's mother is – she'd criticize her and try to 'rescue' her, and Ann would lose all her independence and self-respect, and her mother wouldn't love her!*

Ann's Self, after gently asking the hard worker not to call the other part names, might offer the same question to the comfort-seeking firefighter who might reply: *I'm afraid that the hard worker will work Ann to death for no good reason, because nothing is ever good enough for her mother, and she'll never feel lovable and successful. So I sit her down in front of the telly whenever I can, just to make her stop.*

Once they've both said their piece, you will warmly validate both parts, appreciating them for how they serve the system, as well as appreciating them for their honest and courageous communication. Ask if they've heard what each other has shared and enquire about the effect that has had on each of them. And that's all there is to it – at this stage, there's no need for either part to change its behaviour in any way.

Mediating an inner conversation like this can work wonders all by itself. In therapy, I've witnessed very young parts wordlessly move from being across from each other in fear and animosity to standing back to back, taking on the world as a team. Another time, parts came and stood next to each other and clasped hands; no expectation, just a spontaneous rearranging of the inner family.

Polarization and exiles

Let's not forget the exiles. Polarized parts will be doing what they do to prevent the system from being overwhelmed by the exiled distress of younger parts. If I were working with Ann in therapy, I would gently guide her to ask her polarized parts about their fears, and then (with their permission) guide Ann to be with the part or parts whose distress they are worried about. Based on what you know about IFS so far, you can probably intuit or make an informed guess that Ann's protectors guard an exile (or more than one) who longs for her mother's love, but is burdened by experiences leaving it feeling unlovable, very alone and worthless. That's what I'd suspect myself – but of course we can't know for sure without asking parts directly.

If Ann is doing polarization work on her own at home, she might also sense the exile behind her parts' conflict. While she is in her open-hearted, creative, connected place of Self-energy, something might arise in the inner world that represents the exile and its presently locked-away presence in the system. In the moment inside, if the polarized parts are either side of a table, then there might be a book on a shelf nearby that speaks to the exile's experience of itself, or a painting on the wall. If Ann's parts are seated either side of the fire, then there might be something on the mantelpiece above the fire or on the tile surround at the foot to represent the exile. Such symbols can be subtle hints alluding to the presence of a part protectors won't allow you to approach directly. Knowing of an exile and connecting to it with compassion in such an indirect way can have an impact.

Speaking *for* parts in the external world

Just as we can help our parts communicate more skilfully inside, we can use IFS principles to work with our parts to communicate more effectively with external others. Another way to welcome inner family members and be responsible for them and their impact on others is to speak *for* your parts, not *from* them. Difficult communication with other people often happens when our parts are in charge and using our mouths to speak. The principle of speaking *for* our parts is especially useful when you want to be heard rather than to incite or evoke a reactive part in the other.

Here are various ways in which an elderly member of an external family communicates during Sunday lunch:

- 'Aggh, my foot's cramping. Aggh!'
- 'You know I suffer from cramps, and I need to add salt. Why don't you put it down this end? I remind you every time; no one ever listens.'
- 'Can you pass the salt, please?'

Do you sense which communication might be easiest for others around the table to receive? The first two examples show someone clearly speaking *from* a part: the first, an exile who wants to attract others' care by expressing pain; the second, a manager who's trying to shame others into caring properly. Both parts' communications are likely to activate parts in others. One person's put-upon manager might grumble, *No matter how nice I make things, there's always something wrong. Why do I bother?* Someone else's firefighter might rage inside, *You miserable old codger, why don't you just shut up!* The atmosphere around the table is now a little uncomfortable if not downright awkward and unhappy. On the other hand, the third communication – a simple request for salt – might elicit a neutral or even pleasant Self-led response from others. They might silently pass the salt or even say, 'Sorry, I keep forgetting to put the salt down your end. Here it is.'

Remember, the parts who try to get the salt by hollering in pain or shaming others aren't in the wrong; they have health concerns and are probably experiencing fear of potential pain at night when the next 'cramp attack' happens. Understandably, they have directed that protective energy out onto the external people at the table. If the elderly family member had read this book or had some IFS sessions, their parts might have been able and willing to allow their Self to know their thoughts, feelings and fears. One would have expressed inside the fear of pain, while the other would have grumbled internally about others' neglect, and both would be heard out sympathetically by the elderly person's Self – who would also agree that some salt is needed! Then their energy might naturally have softened enough to allow Self to speak *for* them and their needs at the dining table.

When we have spoken *from* a part – and we all sometimes do – if damage has been done or upset caused in a relationship, it's important we can acknowledge that and apologize on behalf of the part. After parts of them yelled or shamed others at the table, the elderly relative might have said later, with a bit more

Self-energy, 'Sorry I made a big thing about the salt not being in reach; that was a lovely lunch, thank you.'

Refrain from pointing out other adults' parts

Speaking for our own parts often feels good for our system and makes sense to others. However, it's generally not wise to *tell* another person what part of them is driving their inner psychic bus! (Unless you are their therapist, of course – and even then, pointing out someone else's parts takes considerable tact and diplomacy.) Even if we understand that our parts are likely to be young children, when someone else calls out our parts, it can feel shaming inside.

Now that you've learned about IFS, you might be tempted to tell a spouse or partner, 'There's that part of you who's pulling away again!' or 'There's a part of you behaving like a surly teenager.' Such observations are seldom Self-led; it's usually the part of *you* hurt by that behaviour who is pointing it out (with passion). But your understanding of IFS can help you interact with other people's parts more sensitively by paying respectful attention to what *your* parts are noticing.

When someone seems to be speaking *from* a part of their system, and a part of me is activated, I might say inside: 'Okay, we both notice their part. I'm here. Let me be here with you and with this part of them.' That might be sufficient to soothe reactive parts in me. And once my part feels heard, my creative, confident, clear, connected Self-energy stands a much better chance of responding to someone else's behaviour in a way that reduces the likelihood of part-against-part conflict.

My husband, who is also a trained IFS therapist, is adept at being aware of certain of my parts without presuming to notify me about them. When he notices a reactive part of me behind the wheel of my psychic bus, he'll say from a calm place of observation without judgement, 'You seem a bit anxious.' What he's noticed is how short my part's fuse is and how tensely irritable it's making me. Aware that pointing out 'Emma's irritable part' does not usually go well, he recognizes and speaks for the deeper anxiety he senses is likely to be driving its efforts to protect me with a 'fight' response. It seems to work for us; my anxious part feels seen in a non-judgemental way, and both it and my 'fighty' part can relax and ease back from the inner steering wheel.

Point out children's parts with great care

While it's important not to presume to name the parts of other adults without their permission, our flesh-and-blood children may well benefit from a Self-led adult helping them notice the parts of them behind whatever it is they are feeling inside. But as always, curiosity and respect are indispensable. Anna Vincentz, the Danish family therapist and IFS specialist I've quoted before, explains:

> It can be helpful to name things for and try to translate our children's behaviour, as it can help them feel seen and help them get more of a language (and thereby cognitive understanding of themselves), which can make the behaviour or physical symptoms unnecessary as a primary means of expression. However, it's important to do this in a curious and open-ended way, where our children can become curious inward and feel free to say no to our speculations or offerings. But what is more important here is that we, as parents, know that the behaviour of our children makes sense. Nothing comes from nothing. (Vincentz and Bubbers, 2023, pp. 242–3)

Journal prompt

Communicating with your parts every day

Here are some ideas for how you can cultivate open lines of communication with your parts as you go through life together from day to day:

- At the start of the day (or the night before) look at your diary or to-do list and get curious about the parts of you that will be involved in churning through that list. Maybe ask if any of them want to confer with Self or each other about the work ahead, or if there is anything they need from you or from other parts of the system.
- At the end of the day, you might take some time to reflect on what has occurred and the parts that were involved. If all went well, can you communicate some appreciation and love to your parts? If things were challenging, can you communicate some compassion and understanding?
- If during the day or at the day's end, a meeting to 'debrief' is needed, how will you do that? Will you gather everyone round inside in your imagination, in writing or by drawing? As you ponder how best to hold meetings, see if anyone inside needs anything of you or wants to share an idea.
- Throughout the day, be curious about any changes you experience in your inner world – if you notice moving from one speed to a slower speed, or from anxious to less anxious or relieved, for example. Consciously communicate with your parts about the change if you can.
- Throughout the day, notice your interactions with other people, and be curious about who comes forward to the driving seat in your inner psychic bus. Which parts of you took the lead in which external communication, and why? How did they feel about how those conversations went? Be sure to enquire in a spirit of openness and curiosity, knowing you are all on the same team.
- If your parts are in distress at any time, communicate clearly that you understand – even if you don't have time for deeper inner enquiry. Get curious about anyone inside who is not okay. If you cannot meet with them immediately, let them know you remember them and that they are not on their own inside (even if it feels that way right now).

Section 4
TROUBLESHOOTING

9

When IFS isn't working

A decade ago, when I first learned the Internal Family Systems model, it was little practised among psychotherapists in the USA and almost unheard-of in the UK. Today the word is out, and IFS certainly seems to be the fastest-growing therapeutic method worldwide. At present, there are nowhere near enough trained IFS therapists and practitioners to meet the growing global demand, which means most people now begin their journey into the model without one-on-one professional support. In fact, I imagine most readers of this book are using it to explore their inner families on their own.

This chapter and the next will be especially helpful for do-it-yourselfers, as they address the most common challenges people and their parts encounter when they're making a start with IFS (and getting curious). I encountered all these problems myself when I was new to my internal family; my therapy clients encounter them as well, and so do the psychotherapists I support as a clinical supervisor. So if you're experiencing difficulties exploring your inner world, this section of the book will give you some clues, answers and food for thought.

Please note that I may not have headed the different sections in the way you would when coming here for help with whatever difficulty you are having. It is worth scanning through the following pages to locate a heading that might best fit with what you are experiencing. Even if what I write doesn't directly relate, there may still be something – a principle or tip, for instance – that proves useful. It is worth persisting; I've got lots to share.

When parts don't respond to standard IFS language or practices

The version of IFS you've been learning in this book is what I might call 'plain vanilla', the model as it is taught by Richard Schwartz and the IFS Institute. Even so, an experienced IFS practitioner would be able to detect an unmistakable Emma Redfern flavour in it. That is because we all adapt the model to suit our systems and, for professionals, the systems of our clients. If the terms and concepts in this book are broadly appealing but do not seem to work when you turn inward, the problem might not be IFS as such, but rather the specific words and practices in which you have learned it.

If that's the case, I encourage you and your parts to create a bespoke version of IFS, one that works perfectly just for your system. That is what IFS professionals like me do with our clients: we adapt the model, in the moment, to the needs of their particular parts. Shawnee Schmid, a counsellor of children and young people in Australia, has written about how she adapts 'vanilla' IFS to suit the needs of the young people she works with (Schmid, 2023). Sometimes, she changes the language of 'sensations' to 'body clues'. The idea of 'fleshing out' a part becomes 'finding out more', to avoid zombie connotations! 'Target part' might become 'focus part'. Your parts will help you make similar adjustments if you listen to how they respond to your Self.

If you are a concrete thinker who takes things literally, as many neurodivergent people do, then the metaphorical language of standard IFS might not work for your system.[1] If the idea of driving an 'inner psychic bus' doesn't work, don't use it – you can find another way of explaining how parts occupy the seat of consciousness. Even the word 'parts' is a metaphor, which your parts might or might not find congenial; it might take some experimentation to hit on the concept that makes sense in your unique system. Here are some alternatives to 'parts':

- Networks of neural connections
- Software programs or apps
- Modes or flavours of experience
- Sub-personalities
- Internal persons.

Unblending and blending might become 'passing the baton' or 'changing channel'. Updating a part about your present life might be explained as 'pressing the refresh button' or 'installing an update'.

Language of 'feeling' in the standard question 'How do I feel towards the part?' might not be right for your system; in that case it's okay to use some other means of testing for the presence of Self-energy. The answers to the following questions will provide an indication of the presence of Self or of a part just as well:

- Is my heart open?
- Am I interested and without an agenda?
- Do I sense warmth and welcome to what's inside?
- Can I extend any of the C qualities to this part at this moment?

Sometimes it's not the language that is the issue, it's more that your system needs a physical or practical cue to assist in accessing Self-energy. Consider using a phrase or mantra, visualizing a calm place in nature, or linking a C quality with a particular movement – compassion with stroking the hands or the arms, for example, or noticing and slowing the breath for calm. These methods can enable some space to open up inside if the usual IFS methods don't suit your parts.

When it's 'just not working'

Paying attention to progress

How well IFS is working for you depends on what your system hopes to achieve. So let's start by asking how you are assessing your IFS journey. Did you write down an intention when you started? Maybe you listed what you hoped to achieve (if anything) out of engaging with your inner world. If you did set such intentions, I encourage you to refresh your memory of them now, so you can clarify how you are hoping IFS will benefit you. Perhaps your goals have changed; if so, perhaps you might update them. Or you might want to set some intentions now that you know a bit more about what the model can do.

If you are anything like me – and many of the clients and therapy professionals I have spent time with – then your parts may be quick to perceive difficulties, and less skilled at noticing progress, positive shifts or interesting changes. If that describes you, you might want to solicit input from trusted people who are close to you and ask them if they have seen progress from your explorations. You may be surprised by what you hear: they may say something like 'You seem less reactive these days' or 'You're back to being playful'.

Beyond input from others, I encourage you to look specifically for signs of change within yourself. Be gently curious as you proceed; see if your system can be open to recognizing progress and benefits, even subtle ones. For example, if a client tells me that he and his mother are now having more comfortable conversations, he might shrug and say, 'I guess she's mellowed with age' – whereas I would point out that his system recently let go of a legacy burden, which might have made it easier to communicate with the parent from whom he'd first inherited it.

If you've been keeping a journal of your IFS journey in some form, as I've recommended, it is worth taking time to go back and review it thoughtfully. You may have made more progress than you think.

Looking for change in more than one place

I wrote earlier that IFS isn't about making our parts change. It's about making introductions between Self and our parts; then magic can happen. It often takes time for our Self to earn the trust of our parts, and it's no use rushing them. Remember the IFS axiom: 'Slow is fast, fast is slow.' Also, it is important not to limit ourselves to looking for signs of change only on the inside. We can notice progress through action in the external world, too – and that is often the focus of therapy or personal growth, to show up or behave differently. For example:

- A person in group therapy feels hurt by other members of the group and, one session, leaves without saying goodbye. Some of their parts assume that 'storming out' means failing at therapy. However, after further inner dialogue, it turns out that, to other parts inside, 'storming out' was a triumph. As a system, they realize in exiting that they are no longer a child trapped in relationships it's impossible to get out of.
- Someone struggles to enter into relationship with their parts, sensing only body tensions when they try to look inside. Over time, they become aware that some of their parts believe *they can't get anything right* and *it's all going to go horribly wrong*, so they shut down the whole endeavour. The client leaves IFS therapy, concluding, 'It's not working.' Around the same time, they decide to take their classic car to pieces to try and get it running again, an avocation they find thoroughly rewarding. Once this person's system encountered the *idea* of being internally complex in therapy, their parts chose to take that knowledge and use it in their own way. Some of their inner team took the occasion to become more noticeable or 'fleshed out' during the car mechanics; the person's Self, now

alert to their presence, notices the parts who delight in this new pursuit. The world doesn't cave in when the car fails to start the first time; they are doing this for the love of it. They experience more spaciousness inside.

- A woman experiencing fatigue has had no success working with parts related to her tiredness – those that fear it, working-hard parts who might be causing it, and so forth. A health check-up surfaces a physical problem that, once rectified medically, brings renewed energy and clears the brain fog. Taking careful notice of her inner world, she was able to determine that her parts weren't using her fatigue to communicate after all – her fatigue had a biological cause, which she could and did take action to treat.

- After decades of trying to be a 'good enough husband', a man in his seventies realizes that the changes wanted by his system are not possible through having therapy. Guided by a consensus among his parts, he walks out of an unfulfilling marriage and soon finds someone else to share his life with who wants to value him as he is.

What do your parts make of the above examples? Perhaps your inner world is evolving in ways you can see *outside* yourself. Maybe someone inside is speaking up to say it's a good idea to see a medical or alternative practitioner. Perhaps there are voices suggesting it's time to find an IFS professional to bring increased Self-energy and momentum to your inner explorations.

Who says, 'It's not working'?

If there's a part of your system saying *It's not working*, it's worth getting curious about who that is. Remember, Self doesn't have an agenda for something to work, so it's unlikely these words are being spoken by the you-who's-not-a-part. If you can sense the part holding this belief, in or around your body or in your mind, and you can access curiosity and a feeling of acceptance, extend those towards the frustrated part. Ask it to tell you more. You might enquire, 'What were you hoping for?' Follow your curiosity and creativity and build a relationship with this part, welcoming any disappointment, frustration, fear and more. Your conversation, your Self might gently point out, suggests that it *is* working after all.

You might even find that a sceptical or pessimistic part has an investment in inner work *not* working. They might feel duty-bound to keep performing their current role, or they might fear losing an important external relationship if too much were to change. If you have a sense that parts of you have similar invest-ments in the status quo, the you-who's-not-a-part could address any fears you hear in response to the question, 'What are you afraid would happen if IFS were to work?'

Remember, coming to know a protector like this might bring your attention to another part of your system, one who is exiled for the common safety and good. If that exiled energy and distress do arise, you can ask protectors to give you space to be present for it with compassion, curiosity, presence and welcome. Assure everybody that there is no agenda for changing or doing differently, just being with the exile, com-municating to the exile that you care for it. And if that proves especially difficult, it may be time to seek the support of an IFS professional to help you guide your system through the steps of healing.

Doubt and scepticism are excellent invitations to get curi-ous about who in your inner world is speaking. Be as curious as you can. *I'm never going to get it right, what an idiot!* could be spoken by a criticizing part – *or* by the part who feels criticized. How your Self responds will depend on who's saying that inside, and why. If it's a critical manager part, trying to protect you by shaming you into better behaviour, you might say kindly, 'Thank you for trying to help, I'll take it from here.' To an exiled part who feels crippled by past experiences of criticism, you might respond with equal kindness, 'I'm sorry you've been hurt in this way. I love you just as you are.'

When it seems you have no Self

In IFS circles, Self is sometimes called our 'birthright' – not, I think, because it is something we deserve, but because it is something we have as part of human existence. Humans are 'designed', as it were, to house Self-energy, to experience Self-energy in others, and to experience Larger Self, the transcendent Self. Human systems are also designed to protect our survival at any cost – even at the cost of forgetting our Self. Under traumatic enough external circumstances, our protectors push Self out of the body and actively block its return. If that feels right to you, you might consider seeking professional support from a bodyworker trained in IFS or an IFS therapist specializing in trauma.

The good news is that for most people – even those of us who've experienced considerable trauma in our lives – Self is accessible without professional support. If your most prominent parts think you have no Self at all, be curious and actively reflect on your life for times when you have already experienced the qualities of Self: curiosity, calm, creativity, confidence, clarity, courage, compassion, connectedness. Recalling such moments can help our parts warm up to the idea that Self, the source of such joyful experiences, is still readily available inside.

When I was making a start with IFS, my parts found certain memories of Self especially helpful. One was at university after graduation – I was the first female graduate to get a first in my subject for nearly two decades. There was an after-party in my department, and I recall feeling free, in the moment and safely embodied; I could access calm, confidence, clarity, and enjoy connectedness with those faculty and students with whom I had spent the last three years and whose families had come to join us in celebrating and to mark the occasion. Reflecting on that moment, my hard-working parts realized that, when they could at last relax and bask in their achievement, the qualities of the Emma-who's-not-a-part shone brightly. A second example of embodied Self-energy came when my husband and I had our first date. It was summer, and, at his suggestion, we went to the beach and hired the necessary kit so that he could introduce me to bodyboarding. Wow! Is there anything like being in the sea for accessing presence, playfulness and connectedness?

Who says 'There is no Self'?

If your system suspects that there is no Self inside, it's a great time to get curious. Try the following and see if it helps. I invite you to invite the sceptical part who turned to this section to take up more space inside of you. Invite them to blend so their energy is noticeable inside, as is how they inhabit and maybe use your body. Then invite the part to read these words I've written especially for them:

> Hello there!
>
> I'm glad you're here, and I'm sorry if this process of inner enquiry feels frustrating and disappointing. (I can't be sure how you are feeling, so I'm guessing here; whatever you are feeling is going to make sense.) Here is what I want to say to you in response to your belief that your system has no Self:
>
> It makes sense that you can't or don't want to believe in the existence of something you've not seen or consciously experienced. I get how doing new things can feel scary or impossible. You may have tried all sorts of things before without success and don't want to get your hopes up again, only to have them dashed. This makes sense, and I'm sorry that's how it's been.
>
> 1. Perhaps you are saying 'There is no Self' from a place of scepticism or dislike of the 'woo-woo' or unconventional nature of IFS as it might seem to you. I understand that. Did you read how some

of my parts responded to Dick Schwartz in the demonstration session? Scepticism is a valuable quality, and we are not asking you to ditch it. In fact, responding to thoughtful doubt has led many people to invest time and money in clinical trials and pilots to create an evidence-base for IFS's efficacy. That might go some way to reassure parts like you. But you must judge for yourself. We invite you to be open to the *possibility* that Self might exist, while staying precisely as sceptical as you are. Your rigorous questioning is indispensable.

2. As a psychotherapist and IFS practitioner with many years' experience, I want to offer you my informed opinion: I firmly believe that the system to which you belong has a Self. In my clinical and personal experience, everyone is born with a Self which cannot be damaged or destroyed. You are welcome to choose to trust me on this for a while, while you investigate the idea for yourself.

It's up to you whether you risk giving space for Self (or another part) to be present and available as a healing presence and resource for you and the rest of your system. Self is not going to push past you and demand you listen or notice. It's up to you to give space for an accepting, welcoming, open-hearted, loving presence to emerge, for you to get to know. The risk is yours to take or not, and we are not about to rush you.

Bye for now,

Emma

Now check inside somehow and see what you notice. Is your sceptical part re-energized, or has it softened a little so there is more space alongside it? In your own way, have you been able to regain the steering wheel of the inner psychic bus? Depending on what you find inside, let your Self take the conversation from there.

When parts feel hopeless

Self doesn't 'do' hopelessness. Many therapists generally lightly hold hope and optimism on behalf of their clients. We 'believe in' our client's abilities to self-heal, to turn a corner or whatever phrase we prefer. In time, our clients can become able to feel hope for themselves and their circumstances. The global pandemic and major changes and challenges in world politics since 2020 to date have challenged this aspect of the therapist's role as it can be hard to hold hope when the state of the world feels hopeless, whether in terms of extreme politics, war, genocide, global warming, racism, transphobia and so on. In IFS there is a special term for how IFS professionals offer IFS-informed hope to parts: being 'the hope merchant'.

> ## The hope merchant
> Being a hope merchant in IFS means holding and sharing the confident, clear and courageous belief that Self is available to everyone, a faith we derive from knowing in our bones that our parts' extreme and distorted beliefs can lose their power and be released in the presence of Self (Schwartz and Sweezy, 2020, pp. 199–200). IFS practitioners like me act as 'hope merchants' for our clients' parts; if you are working with the model on your own, resources like this very book help your parts 'buy into hope' for themselves (see Redfern, 2023b, pp. 181ff).

When what's happening inside doesn't make sense

When we're just making a start exploring inside, and things feel confusing and 'stuck', it might be the case that a part we aren't aware of needs our Self's attention. That can happen when we assume we know who is speaking, when we don't, or if we are unaware of one member of an inner relationship, particularly one side of a polarization.

One way to bring hidden parts to light is to get curious about your parts' frustrations with you. If a part of you is vehement about something, like going to the gym, and yet you cannot make it there, then it is very likely there is at least one other part in your system who wants something else or even the opposite – a part you haven't yet met, perhaps, or one you're not expecting to have an opinion about gym-going. Be curious inside. See if you can meet the part or parts who prefer staying home with the cat, dog or TV. If the part who does *not* want to go to the gym doesn't flesh out fully straight away, see if you can begin to notice it. You might notice it via thoughts like *Do I have to?* Or by feelings or body sensations that communicate, *I'm feeling too self-conscious for the gym today*, or *I'm so tired!* It might be noticeable by its actions: when you leave your gym kit at home (yet again), or when you 'accidentally' double-schedule the dentist – *Which is way more important, and the gym will still be there tomorrow.*

Other parts of your system might be hard to perceive because the cultural or legacy burdens they bear make your system try to hide them. It is inevitable that through living in whatever society you are living in – that's Western industrialized, capitalist society for me – some parts will be more 'acceptable' in society than others. Those who feel unacceptable – or who are told they are by other parts – may well be hidden or exiled. For example, the media, the medical profession and our families may put pressure on us to make our body a certain shape and size. We may have parts who are burdened by spoken or unspoken dictates such as *Thin is best* or even *Being fat is shameful.* Those inside who *like* to be in a larger body may not be heard from and known directly; to all intents and purposes, they are hidden from our awareness. But, of course, hidden parts still affect the system, and the actions we take: for reasons that mystify our manager parts, we may find that dieting just does not last, and those curves break out again as a part who likes and wants them takes control of the inner steering wheel for a time.

Remember, this is your inner family we are talking about – your inner tribe, gang, team, or whatever term you use. They are your community, and they all matter. So be curious and open to getting to know *everyone* who wants to be known. Make sure it's your Self in the driving seat when you do, though. If you find yourself searching for a hidden part with an urgent 'fix it' or 'sort it' mentality, then that's another part at work, not your Self. You can hear out that part's concerns and, when it's ready to, it can let the you-who's-not-a-part lead the search party. If the more talkative part in a polarization objects, you can reassure it: 'I'm not going to take sides; I'm interested in meeting and coming to know all parts involved. I love and value all of my parts; you are all welcome.'

When inner enquiry feels overwhelming

While exploring your inner world with IFS can be profoundly healing and liberating, it can also be challenging. Our Self may ask our parts to take risks that feel quite daunting: trusting Self when external others have proven untrustworthy, allowing exiled parts to share potentially overwhelming feelings, letting go of burdens that feel indispensable. Inner enquiry requires considerable mental and emotional energy, especially at first.

Life being what it is, our systems sometimes simply do not have any energy to spare. If your parts feel IFS isn't working right now, that might be because they need all their energy to manage the conditions of your *external* world. Perhaps life is especially challenging, and your parts are giving everything they've got just to hold your life together. That's understandable. If you're going through something big in the external world, your parts might need you to let them keep doing their jobs without you 'interrupting' until you've got to the other side.

If that's the case, share hope inside: life will not always be so hard, and Self is *always* here to love and support every part, even while they're working hard. Even if your protectors can't stop what they're doing for long enough to support inner exploration, your Self has their backs on the inside, right now, always. And you can come back to IFS whenever the time feels more agreeable.

Journal prompts

Reflecting on your access to Self-energy

In **Chapter 3**, I suggested you get curious about when and where you have accessed any of the C qualities, the P qualities or the AWOLs. Often, the qualities of Self become apparent to us spontaneously and without effort, in the presence of natural beauty, human frailty, a loving other (four-legged or human) and so on.

- Copy out the diagram (Figure 9.1: The 8 Cs) on a bigger scale, or use this one, and jot down some memories of the Self-qualities you remember from your own experience.
- Write down times you have experienced any of these qualities in another person.

Teasing out trailheads from past experiences

As you may have realized, you cannot befriend parts that are out of awareness. If you are up for it, here is an idea to tease out trailheads which might lead you to parts relevant to this chapter and IFS 'not working'.

With your curiosity to the fore, reflect on when you have experienced the *opposite* of a quality of Self-energy, Self-leadership or the AWOLs. Here are the steps with an example below:

1. Choose a C, P or AWOL quality of Self.
2. Determine what you think is the opposite of the quality you've chosen – whatever feels right to your system. For you, the opposite of *connectedness*, for example, might be *hostility, isolation, rejection* or something else.
3. Check inside for any concerned parts and address any fears they have about getting curious about this anti-quality. If necessary, agree upon a safety plan. This might be as simple as having one of your protectors monitor the exercise and stop it in case of trouble. Send your protectors some appreciation, and remind them that parts have the ability not to overwhelm Self.

4. Let your mind focus on that opposite quality. You might feel a little of it in your body, thoughts might arise, or you might focus with gentle curiosity on a time when you experienced this opposite. Notice what comes up from a place of curiosity and compassion.

5. Send some appreciation to your system and let the you-who's-not-a-part respond as seems fitting in this moment.

6. Then, without becoming overwhelmed, and using what you have learned about IFS so far, follow the trailhead a little way until you find a part (or parts) who made a 'rule for living' in response to the opposite quality that just revealed itself.

7. Be curious as to if and how this showing up now is relevant to any struggles you are having with IFS and to your journey with this book.

Here is an example of how I have used the above enquiry process:

1. I chose the quality: Calm.

2. For me, the opposite would be: Panic.

3. I check for concerns inside about doing this enquiry: None at present.

4. Spontaneously a memory from childhood comes. I recall my sister and I were out on our bikes and crossing a field; the wheels became so gummed up with mud, they stopped turning. (I'm looking on this memory from a distance, not through the first-person perspective of my young self.) I don't recall how my sister responded, but I went into a panicky overwhelmed state, thinking we would *not* be able to get the bikes home. I got so distressed and desperate that I even asked a passing stranger for help. They didn't stop; they kept on walking. I don't recall how any of us got home.

5. I send some appreciation and acknowledgement to my parts: 'That looks so hard for you; I'm sorry you were so scared and overwhelmed.'

6. Yes, at least one part adheres to a 'rule for living' bolstered by that experience: *In times of trouble, you're on your own; no one's going to help.* To which another part pipes up: *We're not on our own, we have books.*

7. A 'go-it-alone' rule for living has often kept my system from asking for support while also being instrumental in my becoming an author of IFS books: my system doesn't want anyone to feel alone in times of struggle with the model.

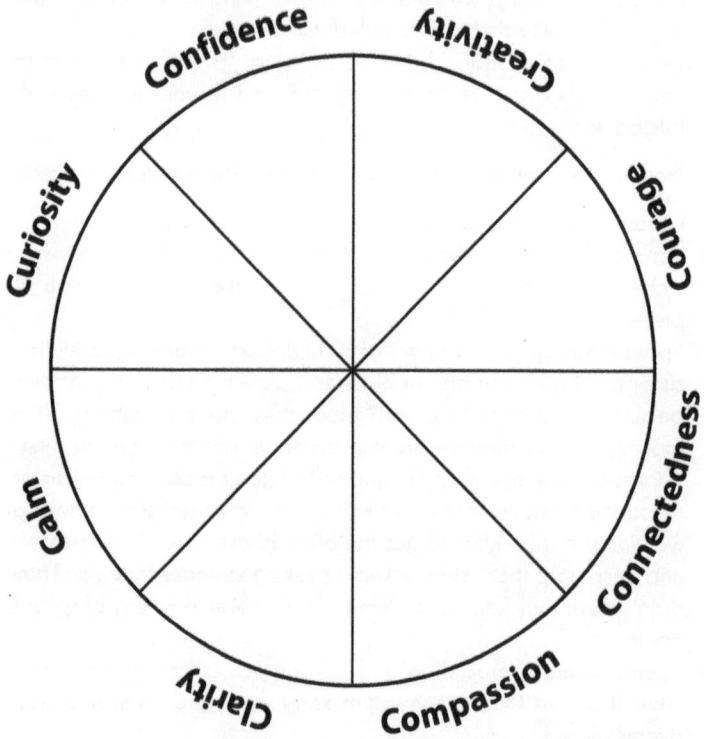

Figure 9.1 The 8 Cs

10

When IFS is working too well

In the previous chapter, we explored some common ways inner enquiry can run into trouble. In this chapter, I offer guidance about how to respond when IFS *is* working – perhaps too well for your system's comfort! Meeting your Self for the first time, realizing they're not alone and never have been, getting to know other parts: for the members of your inner world, these are momentous and world-changing events, which often provoke strong reactions. After years of experience in my own system and my clients, I've learned about many of the different reactions you may experience on going inside.

Even if you've come here with a specific difficulty in mind, it's worthwhile reading this whole chapter, since guidance offered in one section may well turn out to be relevant as you continue your IFS journey. Here again, I write mostly for those of you working on your own; if you are using IFS together with a friend, family member or professional practitioner, feel free to adapt as needed.

When many parts arrive at once

When you first turn your attention inward, lots and lots of your parts might immediately begin clamouring for your attention all at once. They may rush forward pell-mell because they are eager or even desperate to meet Self, or concerned to prevent Self from meeting another part. Your mental conversation might sound like a deafening roar. Alternatively, your parts might talk to you in rapid succession, even as your internal speech or stream of thought flows smoothly – so smoothly, perhaps, that it might seem that just one part is speaking, but making no sense at all. For example: *I hate this illness, and it's not fair. Thank goodness I don't have to go to that event later – oh, I'm always disappointing people! I'll never feel normal again ...*

However you experience a crowd of parts, a confusing inner cacophony can seem like an insurmountable barrier to doing an inner enquiry. It may feel particularly discouraging to parts who want IFS to bring wholeness, healing and improved mental health. Don't give up, though: there are things you can try.

Asking parts to come one by one

If you've You-turned inside and see, hear or sense a crowd of parts coming at you, you can quickly address them all at once. Because most of our parts are quite young, it might be helpful here to consider what you would say if a group of children were to rush at you. I might say, for example, something like this: 'It's great you are all here! I intend to meet and be with each of you over time. To do that, I need to be able to pay careful attention, which I can't if you all talk to me at once. I promise I will get to know you in time, just one by one, please. So, see if you can hold back a little – you'll work out how – to determine who needs to come forward first.'

Addressing the system over a loudspeaker

If your parts are too rowdy to listen to such a request, you can simply turn your attention back outward again and try again later on. To begin your next attempt, it's worth being pre-emptive. *Before* you start looking round your inner world for your parts, speak to anyone who might be inside over what I think of as an internal public broadcast or loudspeaker system. My announcement might go like this:

Hi, everyone. I've set aside ten minutes to learn about my inner world this morning. Instead of coming inside right away, I'm going to talk to you in my head for a while like this. Any of you that want to listen, please do; if not, you're welcome to go about your business. Here goes: hello and welcome! I know this IFS business might seem new and strange to some of you. I appreciate you showing up and, in the hope of making things easier for all of us, I want to explain something. When you're speaking to me all at once, I can't hear any of you well, so I don't get to be with you. I'm wondering if together we can come up with some way of you making yourselves known that is less overwhelming for me.

You can carry on like that, being as open, curious and creative as your system allows; some ideas for what to say will come, just look out for them. Because many of your parts really do want to be known, they usually get the wisdom of figuring out how to approach you one by one – or at least in manageable pairs or threes.

When a part overwhelms the system

Speaking of overwhelm – and this may sound counterintuitive – most of our parts can *choose* how much they overwhelm or 'hijack' the system in any given moment. Again, because they *want* to be known by you, they will gladly adjust how they approach you so they can be. Parts usually don't know that they can modulate their own intensity this way, so you can tell them. Learning of this almost magical ability often brings great relief system-wide.

Showing parts how to lower their intensity

To help your parts learn how to dial down their intensity, you can furnish a physical device for doing so in your inner world. Some parts like the idea of a literal dial they can use to reduce or amplify their own intensity or blending. The intensity-modulation device you furnish for a part should suit its age and tastes; a teenage part might like turning a volume knob on a radio, while a grown-up manager might use a smartphone app. No matter what device you come up with together, it is often helpful to demonstrate how the dial works by inviting the part to turn their intensity *up* one tick, then *down* two ticks.

Parts can adjust the intensity of their communication with you in many other ways, too. Parts can move farther away or come closer to your Self at will. They can build special-purpose rooms, as you read earlier, to contain some of their intensity, or so other parts aren't frightened they will take over. If they don't want to address your Self directly, or can't do so without overwhelming you, they can communicate with you by telephone or over a radio. Those are just some ideas; I am regularly amazed at the inventive intensity-modulation tactics parts come up with as soon as they learn such a thing is possible.

When parts don't show up

Some people experience the opposite problem: instead of a crush of eager parts, they turn inward and encounter what appears to be no one at all. That experience can be deeply demoralizing, but take heart. In IFS we often say, 'What's *in* the way *is* the way.' Just as Self welcomes all parts, no matter what, Self can also welcome parts who do *not* want to show up or are not ready. Seeking consent, taking parts seriously, and negotiating for contact and communication are important.

'There's no one here'

If, when you turn inward, you find yourself thinking 'There's no one here' with anxiety, despair or frustration, follow up with a simple question: 'Says who?' Seriously. You can safely assume that *any* thought you encounter inside that comes with bad feelings is coming from a part, not from your Self. Remember, Self holds only a light healing agenda and desire for harmony and connection: the you-who's-not-a-part is fearless, endlessly hopeful and serenely without urgency. When you encounter what appears to be a desolate internal landscape, it's often because a well-meaning protector part is trying very hard to do IFS for you – and may be frightening other parts away.

If you recognize this scenario, be curious. If you get some sort of answer to 'Says who?' – even just *I don't know* – then you can proceed to make a gentle approach to whatever part of you said so. If the answer to 'Says who?' is something like *Just me*, you can conclude that an inner protector is driving your psychic bus. That protector – who clearly knows IFS as well as you do, and is likely reading this very sentence – can simply ask itself, *What am I frightened would happen if there weren't any parts in here?* Or, *What do I hope to gain from IFS?* Those questions can help the protector who's in charge recognize that it is blended with you, which in turn might help it voluntarily give space so more Self-energy is available inside.

There's just darkness, fog or nothingness inside

Often the first thing people encounter inside is what feels like nothing: absolute or relative darkness, an impenetrable fog or mist, or even a void or vacuum. As ever, get curious: you can ask if the blackness, greyness, fog or nothingness is a part of you showing up in this way initially. Any sort of answer to that question at all – a subtle shift in the grey, a faint ripple in the fog, or even a clear *No, not a part* – and you can assume that you're interacting with a part and turn to it. If there is no response at all, proceed gently and respectfully, leading with curiosity: 'Did somebody send the blackness or cause it to be here like this?' Be very patient and still as you wait for an answer.

Softly does it in such situations; a part who obscures your inner world undoubtedly has concerns about what would happen if it didn't. Manager parts might be alarmed that going inside and meeting a part would be destabilizing. Firefighters might believe your Self can't handle whatever is hidden from awareness. As gently as you can, address the obscuring part's fears and explore its good intentions, patiently and with generosity.

It might also be the case that the darkness, the fog, the nothingness is an aspect of a part's experience it is revealing to you already. If so, slow down. If a part is showing you *its experience* of inner nothingness, it is likely an exile – so you will need to seek up-front permission from protectors to approach it. If you are working with a practitioner, it might make sense to wait until the next therapy session to approach the part who's sharing nothingness.

When parts show up in uncomfortable ways

Sometimes, parts show up inside or communicate in ways that are hard to tolerate: pain, nausea or stiffness, anxiety or dread. They may respond to Self's presence in ways that feel inconvenient, such as bringing on sleep, deep daydreaming or intense brain fog. Uncomfortable responses to inner enquiry are most often protectors' attempts to keep your system from being overwhelmed by whatever you would encounter if you continued exploring inside. As unpleasant as they might feel in the moment, such strategies make perfect sense to the parts who use them and are well meant.

Sometimes, parts respond to our inner enquiry by evoking distressing images, scary thoughts or traumatic flashbacks which terrify other parts and knock Self out of the inner driving seat. In such cases it is vital to remember, and remind everyone inside, that *Self does not fear parts* – nor does it push scared or scary parts out of the way. If you are up for negotiating with a part who scares others inside, offer to help it find ways to reduce its threat level so that other parts can give space for Self to be present. (It is often helpful to talk with scary parts in secure inner rooms.) Accessing your Self-energy, you can then enquire as usual about the part's positive intention and service to the system. If your system is consistently distressed when you turn inward, or if your parts' distress continues after you return your attention to the outside world, I recommend seeking the services of an IFS professional.

Once you have noticed there is a pattern of uncomfortable inner behaviour blocking access to Self-energy, it might be appropriate to pre-empt it before the next time you attempt going inside. If the discomfort is so intense as to be intolerable, you might try communicating in that general broadcast manner I mentioned in the last chapter: 'Hello! I have set aside some time to pay attention to my inner world. Previously, I haven't been able to do that because someone overwhelms me with nausea (or whatever they do) when I try. In the next couple of minutes, I invite anyone hearing this message to keep whatever or whoever is "too much" to witness out of sight, so I can get to know and be with at least some of our inner world. Until shortly, thank you!' When your protective parts hear that you share their concerns about overwhelm, they might not find it necessary to scare you off this time.

If the discomfort you encounter when you look inside is bearable, your Self can respond to the part who's trying to protect you like so:

- Communicate to the system what you have noticed.
- Offer a welcome and appreciation for the part and its service to the system.
- **Introduce your Self**, and your lightly held intentions for inner healing and harmony.
- Inform the system of the **consequences** of the discomfort that has become noticeable – for example, that frightening mental images knock Self out of the driving seat and block curiosity.

- Suggest the part communicates in a way that is less uncomfortable or distressing to other parts, or to the body.
- If other parts have already met your Self, perhaps suggest that they could provide some sort of character reference for you to the parts who have concerns.
- Explain that, if a part has started a physical or psychological symptom, then it has the power to reduce its intensity or stop it altogether, if it wants to. (Refer to the intensity-modulation strategies earlier in this chapter.)
- Offer to address any fears parts have directly. Make an offer to negotiate and mediate between parts in conflict or who might be scared of each other.

Introducing your Self

In our systems, a part often lives in its own isolated world, entirely unaware of the existence of other parts or Self. Even if some parts know you, others might not. How can you reassure a part your Self is meeting for the first time that you come in peace? It helps to introduce your Self deliberately, in words, gestures or rituals. If a part is particularly wary, it might take many friendly reintroductions, consistently repeated over time. Make sure to say explicitly that you are not simply another part of the system, nor are you like people who have hurt them in the past or in the present. As you get to know more of your inner team, you will start to notice what brings calm and possibility to parts in meeting you.

Consequences

If you are an adult, young parts of you can use over-age activities, including dangerous or risky ones, to do their jobs. Your inner little ones, in all innocence, sometimes figure out ingenious ways of using your adult body and mind to accomplish their goals for your safety: taking alcohol or other substances, for example, or prompting gambling, sexual compulsivity or overwork. On enquiry, all such activity is going to make sense inside. Yet don't assume the young part who uses the extreme behaviour is aware of the consequences to the system and the body, such as hangovers, loss of friends, potential or actual health issues, and so forth. By the time such consequences ensue, *other* parts of the system are usually in the driving seat, and it falls to them to try to repair the damage. Self-leadership involves being accountable for *all* of who and how we are, and includes negotiating limits and boundaries with our parts to preserve our overall safety and comfort in the inner and outer world.

A word about boundaries with other people's parts

Self welcomes all parts no matter what; it does not welcome all behaviour no matter what. If you are assisting someone else as they explore their own system, their parts might show up in a way that leaves *your* parts feeling scared, uncomfortable, or powerless. In that case, it is okay *not* to continue; indeed, it may well be wise to stop until your system has more access to Self-energy. Your Self can also provide limits and boundaries for the parts of the other person who trouble your own. For example, the you-who-is-not-a-part can actively welcome someone else's part's anger, while firmly insisting that you won't tolerate being sworn or shouted at. Another person's parts may have experienced sexual wounding, for example, for which you can have compassion – without agreeing to hear details that your parts would find alarming. By communicating to the other as gently as possible from your Self, and watching carefully for any of your parts who might want to 'help' by blaming and shaming, you can protect your own system and potentially the other person's, too.

Of course, other people's parts can upset yours even if you aren't doing IFS together, simply in the course of everyday life. The same principles apply: while you won't point out someone else's part as such without their permission, you can absolutely be aware of its presence, implicitly affirm and welcome it, *and* firmly set boundaries about its behaviour to protect your own internal family.

I recognize that this is more easily said than done. Sometimes we overlook boundary-setting because our parts think our IFS knowledge, or someone else's, should automatically result in good behaviour. Our parts often employ 'if onlys' against themselves – and others:

- *If only I had more Self-energy, this person's behaviour wouldn't bother me.*
- *If only you had more Self-energy, then you would act in ways that don't make me uncomfortable.*

If you notice your parts using the idea of Self in that way, gently point that out to them and offer to help determine how to set appropriate boundaries together.

When parts revert to 'being in therapy'

I came to IFS after long experience with other forms of psychotherapy, as many people do. If your system has become used to a different kind of therapeutic approach, your parts might automatically respond to your internal enquiries as though they were 'in therapy' with your Self, whatever that means to them.

Many of our parts have learned that 'therapy' means little more than offloading, venting or generally sharing their narrative or story, thoughts, feelings and emotions with a therapist or other trusted listener. There's nothing wrong with this per se. Parts do this in the hope that one day they will feel better, and sometimes they do. But sometimes simply sharing experience with someone else is like running to nowhere on a perpetual treadmill. If you think you have a part caught in this trap (perhaps a part who narrates the events of the day), see if it will have an honest conversation with you about the differences between IFS and other forms of therapy. See what your part might need from you to adapt to the IFS ways, of working; there are plenty of podcasts, meditations and YouTube videos out there if they want to see what they are letting themselves in for.

How IFS practitioners help clients adjust

IFS is an introspective way of engaging with ourselves, which some of our parts may struggle with – particularly if they are used to using therapy simply to vent. As a practitioner and a clinical supervisor, I encounter that phenomenon all the time.

Consider this example from Evie, a pretend IFS therapist I am supervising. Her client Ruby, recently single, has a job she loves that barely covers her bills. She looks in on two ageing parents, for whom she can never get it right, and she dreads the day they will need more care from her. All the while she is actively seeking a new partner to make life easier for herself, but dating is much more difficult and triggering than she expected. Her weekly therapy hour consists of offloading about the week: Ruby's latest caring and dating experiences, her failed attempts at securing a new job. Evie, an IFS practitioner, is struggling to entice her to turn inward rather than just telling stories.

Somewhere towards the end of one therapy session, Evie asks Ruby (for the thousandth time), 'Now you've shared all that, who needs or wants attention inside?'

Ruby sighs. 'I'm not getting the hang of this parts thing,' she says (also for the thousandth time). Ruby doesn't say so, but she is contemplating leaving therapy and saving her money.

When Evie asks my advice about this frustrating case, I know just what to say: 'I'm curious if Ruby's parts are overly invested in change happening in the outside world, rather than on the inside.'

That's the ticket. During their next session, Evie takes a new approach with her client. Rather than sitting and nodding along as Ruby narrates the external details of her life, Evie starts the session by asking Ruby point-blank about any fears her parts might hold about really giving IFS a go. To both women's surprise, they list a number of quite reasonable concerns:

- getting it wrong;
- embarrassing herself;
- not knowing how to do it;
- IFS being too emotionally difficult; and, most importantly,
- inner enquiry might make Ruby give up on finding a new partner to care for her, and she will end up alone.

Although no specific parts take credit for these worries, Ruby's system overall seems delighted not to feel judged or rejected once these fears are out in the open. Evie, sensing an opening, sets to work as a hope merchant. After addressing the simpler concerns, she answers the last and most difficult question: will IFS mean Ruby won't want a partner any longer? Evie explains that Ruby's Self will be the primary **attachment figure** for all her parts inside, which will relax their sense of urgency about finding a partner in the outside world.

Ruby's parts are intrigued by this idea, though highly sceptical. Pursuing her advantage, Evie suggests going inside as an experiment – just to notice how it goes. It goes surprisingly well: a young schoolgirl part shows up and confides in Ruby that she is afraid of being all alone. The time inside feels well spent, and Ruby is eager to return to the young schoolgirl in future sessions.

If your parts, like Ruby's, are invested in changing others or things in the outside world, that does not mean they are doing or thinking anything wrong. Could you be a merchant of hope spreading the word that they have an ally in Self inside who has healing qualities and abilities?

Attachment figure

You may be familiar with the term 'attachment figure' from social media, where attachment theory is recently popular. You might have learned to recognize your own attachment dynamics using words such as avoidant, anxious or 'disorganized'. You may even have a sense of how your early years inform your adult relationships, particularly intimate and romantic ones. IFS brings attachment theory inside: it teaches that Self is the primary and ideal attachment figure for our parts. This view of attachment takes immense pressure off our external romantic partners, who can feel freer and more intimate. Being in connection with Self increases our felt sense of safety, capacity, and connectedness on the inside – which makes us a much 'better' partner on the outside.

When parts are stuck in conflict inside

Sometimes turning inward with IFS can make you aware of an intense polarization between parts – and that awareness can sometimes lock the parts involved into even deeper conflict. If you are feeling stuck inside, remember to look out for and get curious about internal opposing parts or teams of parts. My IFS colleague Holly Stoppit, a dramatherapist and creator of 'Clown-o-therapy', has written about this dynamic in a very helpful way.

In the run-up to delivering an online workshop for the British Association for Dramatherapy (BADth), which her system considers a big deal, Holly was a wreck of nerves and fear. She lets us behind the scenes to listen in on a conversation between two of her trusted protectors, Inner Perfectionist and Master Procrastinator:

> INNER PERFECTIONIST: OK, Holly, it's time to sit down and work on your session plan again. No pressure, but I just want you to bear in mind that it needs to be totally perfect in every way. This is a Big Gig, Holly, it's the BADth conference with all the proper dramatherapists

who write books and papers, and they are giving YOU a platform for the first time. So there needs to be the perfect balance of theory and practice and the delivery needs to be absolutely spot on. OK? Let's go!

MASTER PROCRASTINATOR: I've got an idea! Why don't you just have a little look at what the other presenters are offering, just to check what you're up against. Then maybe you can google some of them and watch some YouTube clips of them talking about their stuff, that'll be inspiring won't it? Then perhaps you could watch a few funny cat videos cos you will have earned that!

INNER PERFECTIONIST: No, no! We haven't got time for funny cat videos. Holly has got to spend every minute working as hard as she can!

MASTER PROCRASTINATOR: OK I can help with that: let's make a cup of tea, then let's maybe pop out to the shop to get some biscuits ...

INNER PERFECTIONIST: Gah![1]

If you are just starting out with IFS, you can easily get stuck listening to such inner arguments repeat ad nauseam – simply because your parts haven't learned that your Self has the ability to intervene.

Fortunately, it can. Holly explains that she slowed down, noticed inside and spotted there were polarized parts at play; she gave them her pen and journal so they could express themselves. She 'listened with compassion and attended to their concerns and when they'd both felt heard and seen, they calmed down enough to let me see who they were protecting'. Beneath their busy conflict was a little girl who grew up in the circus, 'all bright and shiny and able to wow audiences'. Though she didn't know it, the little one was dyslexic. She thought she was stupid and worked hard at 'work-arounds' to disguise her trouble with reading. The Perfectionist was protecting this girl by making sure Holly performed so flawlessly that no one would ever suspect her dyslexia; the Procrastinator, meanwhile, wanted to spare the little one the distress of having to work with reading and writing altogether.

'I gathered all three parts into my heart,' Holly writes, 'and took the lead on the preparation, inviting them to chip in at opportune moments.' Rather than passively listening to her polarized parts argue, Holly invited them into relationship with her Self, helped them speak honestly about the little girl they were protecting, and welcomed all three of them to work on the presentation together, while her Self took the lead.

Like Holly, you can help polarized parts get 'unstuck' by taking a compassionate leadership role. As she describes so vividly, you can take on the role of directing your inner medley of creatives.

How to help polarized parts get unstuck

Time for a summary about working with parts in conflict. While accessing sufficient Self-energy:

- Notice and communicate with parts on both sides of the conflict.
- Get curious about and address their fears; invite them to tell you about any vulnerable exiles they are protecting.
- Help parts grasp each other's positive intentions. (Holly's Perfectionist and Procrastinator both want to make sure no one suspects the little girl's dyslexia, so she won't have to feel stupid.)
- Appreciate all parts equally, and ask for their trust in your Self's capacity to lead.
- If there is a wounded young part behind your protectors' conflict, consider seeking out an IFS practitioner to facilitate a direct relationship between your Self and the little one.

Journal prompt

Taking a break from IFS – you're worth it

In a capitalist society, almost all of us have parts that are burdened by the noxious belief that *I only deserve to exist when I am working hard.* That cultural burden can turn even our efforts to heal inside into endless toilsome labour.

So put the book down, let it go – for now. Take time off and away from IFS. Go have some fun – preferably, the sort of fun where no parts are going to be up in arms afterwards.

If there are parts who think of you as in urgent need of self-improvement, thank them for their service and give them the rest of the day off.

I'll be with you on the other side with the next chapter.

Section 5

THE BENEFITS OF GETTING CURIOUS

11

Truth and freedom

This last section of the book takes on a fundamental question: What's in it for my parts to embark on an IFS journey? Each chapter highlights areas of living in which people have perceived significant shifts from engaging with IFS. I include examples of people (including myself) who have experienced beneficial changes with regard to:

- truth and freedom (this chapter);
- emotional regulation and reduced reactivity (**Chapter 12**);
- self-acceptance and authenticity (**Chapter 13**).

Naturally, there are more benefits than these, but word count and your time are limited! Please note these chapter divisions are somewhat arbitrary; there is often overlap between benefits. For example, the more self-acceptance we have, the more emotionally regulated we become and vice versa.

This next section refers to death by suicide, a highly charged topic for many people's parts. Please consider and enquire inside what your system might need before reading on. If you prefer to skip this bit, you're welcome to stop reading here and pick up the text again at the heading 'Truths can be released'.

Truth

Chance Marshall is an HCPC-registered therapist, clinical supervisor and co-founder of Self Space. I follow him on LinkedIn and read his posts. On 8 October 2024, he reminded us that every day in the UK, 18 people die to suicide. He wrote about how each of those 18 people carried a weight that became too much to bear. For me, some of what Chance may be referring to as unbearable weight comes from parts carrying burdened beliefs about who they are and how life is. (If that idea feels particularly potent in your system, you may want to revisit the second of the journal prompts from **Chapter 2**, about bringing curiosity to your burdened parts.)

Parts of ourselves who suggest dying might believe any of the following:

- *Everyone I love would be better off without me.*
- *I'll never forgive myself, it's too much.*
- *Nothing's ever going to change.*
- *I've lost everything, I'm already dead inside.*
- *Death is the only way to stop the pain; the world won't miss me.*
- *I can't cope, I'm going mad.*
- *I can't bear my physical decline; I'd rather go before my body gives out.*
- *No one cares; no one will notice.*
- *If I could just find the 'off switch', I'd have pressed it already.*
- *Stop the world, I want to get off.*

Truth is relative

I can relate, as I have mentioned. After the fire that damaged my flat, the thought arose in my mind – which is to say, a protector had an idea – that driving off the road (I lived near the M25 at the time) would be a swift and easy way to solve the problem of uncontrollably dissolving into a mess of excruciating feelings, which is what I found myself doing post-fire. At the same time, contradictory thoughts and wants came to mind – which I now recognize as a different part or group of parts, thinking *I want to live*. The parts who wanted to live prevailed over the protector who thought death was the only conceivable solution. As a result, I went to see the GP who prescribed antidepressants. If the part with the idea of suicide had been more vocal or dominant, then I might not have been here to write this book.

My system seems to have known, by intuition, that we were more than any part's burdened belief – that even though one of us wanted to die, the rest of us wanted to live. Our parts hold *beliefs* they believe to be *truths*. *I'd be better off dead* is such a belief; so is *Life is still worth living; it's not time to go*. Somehow, it is important to honour *all* of our parts' beliefs, even the burdened ones, and validate them. From that expansive systemic perspective, our Self can reassure a suicidal part that its thoughts and beliefs make sense in the moment, while also communicating that beliefs may not last forever and can change or be released. If a suicidal person at the point of crisis speaks to someone who is successful in negotiating with them to 'sleep on' their suicidal impulse, then a new dawn may bring a weakening of the burdened belief, or even a new truth altogether.

Because our parts have agency, what is true for one part is not true for all. One of the reasons my system so values IFS is because it actively embraces multiple truths, all of which are equally valid inside. It can be profoundly liberating to observe that parts of us want to live *while* other parts of us want to die. We can and do contain multitudes.

Another truth about suicide showed up in my Facebook feed as I was writing this chapter:

> Friendly reminder that suicide prevention isn't just saying 'here if you need to talk!' and posting a hotline number. It's healthcare. It's housing. It's adequate social welfare. It's food security. It's actually being able to access mental health services quickly.

Parts of us who want to die may simply understand the truth of our external life with particular intensity. Our protectors are sensitive to material realities, and they adjust their strategies accordingly. Social power and privilege do not necessarily translate into greater systemic optimism. In Scotland, men are three times as likely to die by suicide as women. In England, males aged 45 to 49 were found to have the highest suicide rates, while in Wales the highest suicide rate was found among males aged 30 to 34 years.[1] I can't help but think that men in the UK are particularly vulnerable to taking on cultural burdens their systems simply cannot bear. People like Chance Marshall are making a difference. Chance's initiatives for and with fathers are reducing the stigma associated with needing places to talk and listen, to be met and heard, which include therapy spaces.

Truths can be released

Because IFS is a truly transformational therapy and life practice, it can help our parts release their truths and find new ones. That's exactly what happened for my system during our session with Dick Schwartz (some of which you will have read earlier in the book). First, a reminder of the usual sequence of the IFS steps of healing:

1 Witnessing
2 Redo
3 Retrieval
4 Unburdening
5 Invitation, and then
6 Integration and appreciation.

At this point, Dick is negotiating with my protectors for permission to proceed to the target or focus part: an exile carrying sadness, which appeared in the form of a vast sea. A part has come in who is afraid that IFS is not going to work and wants it to stop. It doesn't feel I'm listening to it, and Dick offers to speak with it directly.

> DICK: Okay, you're upset with Emma that she won't listen to you. What if I tell you she won't fail?
> SCEPTICAL PART (making raspberry noises and pulling dismissive faces): Does not compute that she won't fail.
> DICK: Where'd you get that idea Emma will fail?
> SCEPTICAL PART: 51 years' worth.
> DICK: You mean she's been failing for 51 years?

SCEPTICAL PART: Yes.

DICK: You tell her that a lot?

SCEPTICAL PART: Yes.

DICK: What are you afraid would happen if you didn't tell her that a lot and criticize her in that way?

SCEPTICAL PART: Other people would see how broken she is.

DICK: Is that the fear – people here will see how broken she is?

SCEPTICAL PART: No, it's that she *is* as broken as I think she is.

DICK: I promise you that's not true – you have a misconception of who she is.

EMMA (shifting from speaking as the part momentarily): The part's really struggling with that.

DICK: Let me keep talking to it … this one that thinks you're so broken.

SCEPTICAL PART: She feels broken. They said, saw and knew she was broken.

DICK: What if they were wrong?

Here Dick is seeding the idea that it's not factual truth that's being talked about here – just a burdening belief:

SCEPTICAL PART: Might break *them* if she wasn't broken. Someone has to be broken.

DICK: Okay, that might've been true at some point for them, she had to be the broken one. But it's not fair to her, though, right?

SCEPTICAL PART: No.

DICK: We can heal this part and prove she's not broken – just their belief. Then you can unload this belief that she's broken and be less mean inside her.

Dick is being a hope merchant for change on the inside through healing the exile.

Truth can change

Each year the IFS Institute holds a global conference. In 2024, it took place live online, with attendees having access to recorded presentations for a period after the live event. This is how I came to watch the presentation of Lara Baden-Semper MSc Clin Psy, BCN, who has lived both in Europe and in Trinidad. In her presentation, Lara speaks of her experience as a neurodivergent mother, biological mother, stepmother, grandmother, sister, daughter, niece, aunt, and 'auntie mother' of young people and adults who find their way to her. Lara lives with chronic physical health problems, including autoimmune issues and a nervous system that grew up in a traumatizing environment. A certified IFS therapist and IFS Institute assistant trainer, she has been offering neurofeedback and IFS for about 15 years.

Entitled 'Exploring Ableism: Healing through Self-Connection and Clarity', Lara's presentation is rich with her lived experience as well as her intellectual journey of exploring and understanding the way **ableism** can be the oppressive force from which all other forms of oppression draw power. She sheds light on the nature of 'normal' – a burdensome concept important to many people's parts, including some in my system – as a socially constructed idea masquerading as universal truth. As someone who grew up in a family with generations of undiagnosed or unsupported autism and ADHD, Lara speaks for the culture of internalized oppression in her own system, including the loud voice in her head who shouts at her when she makes a mistake or forgets something. This voice tells her she *can't get a thing right and messes everything up*, and loudly demands (a refrain common to such parts), *What is wrong with you?* Other inner voices make her feel she is ugly because of her skin colour (she is Black) and distort her sense of herself.

With IFS, Lara tells us, change has come to her system – together with new and different truths. Lara now understands that the berating parts are trying to help by having Lara show up in the world in 'normal' ways they consider crucial to avoid further hurt and rejection – not limping, appearing well, and so on. After much IFS practice, Lara's compassion for these parts has blossomed. She validates the beliefs they hold and communicates that she understands where they come from, while also updating her parts from Self that they are *all* lovable, acceptable and valuable.

Ableism

Rebekah Taussig, a disabled woman and disability scholar, defines ableism clearly: 'the process of favoring, fetishizing, and building the world around a mostly imagined, idealized body while discriminating against those bodies perceived to move, see, hear, process, operate, look, or need differently from that vision' (Taussig, 2020, p. 10).

Monitoring how we might be perceived through an able person's gaze, Lara explains, can be an automatic response of protectors in a disabled person's system. She shares her striving to walk properly without a limp and generally overthinking and 'efforting', which only increases the stiffness, tightness and anxiety in her body whenever she is in public.

I can relate as I have parts who really don't want me to take my back friend (a fold-up mobility aid) on a long train journey. They would rather we suffer back pain than suffer the indignity and shame of needing an aid others will see and that these (apparently 'normal') others themselves don't need and might judge us for. When I met with Lara on Zoom after reaching out to her post-conference, she spoke of a mismatch between the inner perceived truth of her parts and the truth of Self: 'My parts were trying to get me to be viable. They didn't know that we already were.'

IFS offers our parts the opportunity to change what they believe to be true – not because Self convinces them through argument, but because Self's leadership removes the necessity to maintain burdensome old 'truths' for protection. Once Lara's system realized they were *already* 'viable', their sense of the truth changed completely. And with new truth comes freedom.

Freedom

Asking for freedom inside

A client of mine I'll call Zoe will help me explain how IFS brings inner liberation. In her forties, Zoe has recently returned to college to study something completely different from her day job. Understandably, she has been finding the academic side of her course challenging, and although she is quite capable of doing the work, she is struggling to complete her assignments.

In the therapy session, Zoe speaks from many parts who believe burdensome truths:

- *I don't seem to know how to learn.*
- *I need the conditions to be right before I can start studying, and, of course, they never are.*
- *I resent that part who needs things 'just so'.*
- *There's not enough time, so I don't start.*
- *I've got 'comparison-itis'! There are some super-studious students in the group who can just do all this stuff I can't, which doesn't help.*
- *I'm frustrating myself.*
- *I'm frightened of getting it wrong and being made fun of.*
- *Forcing myself to study by having a weekly 'study day' just isn't working.*

I lead us in acknowledging and appreciating the parts involved, reminding Zoe that protectors have positive intentions. I'm also curious about the parts she's not spoken for, who were involved in signing her up for the course and seem pleased about how she's doing in it. Zoe speaks from those parts, too. We also reflect together on her current job, at which she excels, and on other areas of her life in which she is talented. I wonder aloud if anything in any of these other areas, where Zoe's system feels confident, can inform us about 'the problem' of struggling to do her coursework. Zoe seems to like the idea, but I hear some parts dismiss the idea out of hand.

At this point in the session, it's nearing the end. My system has complete clarity that my client has the resources needed to study well, and that her parts are acting as constraints in order to protect her. Rather than working with her parts one by one,

I address the whole system: 'I hear how the parts of you who believe you're incapable of studying are controlling your system.'

The room seems to go still; tears rise, and I hear a marked shift in Zoe's tone of voice. A new part is speaking, perhaps an exile.

ZOE'S CONTROLLED PART: I do feel controlled, I've always felt controlled.

This part of Zoe will need some attention, I know; but for now, I turn back to the whole system to address the problem at hand:

EMMA: Yes, your system has experienced so little freedom. And I'm aware that protectors often get the opposite of what they want – they want to keep you from being ashamed, but they contribute to you feeling not good enough, for example.

ZOE: Uh huh.

EMMA: Remember when you told me earlier that you spontaneously 'did some IFS' earlier today? You asked a teenage part inside who wanted to act all moody with your cousin at lunchtime if it would not take over?

ZOE: Yes. The part was like, 'Sure, no big deal.' My cousin and I had a nice time together.

EMMA: Yes, you asked, and the part gave space willingly. I'm wondering if you could try the same with these parts who have opinions and feelings about studying. Maybe they could let you and the parts who signed up for the course and think you're doing well have some freedom every so often.

ZOE (thoughtfully): This doesn't have to wait until those parts are 'fixed' or 'made to change'; I can just ask them to go away for a bit?

EMMA: Yes, that's it.

ZOE (laughing): I've got a part who wants to tell them to 'fuck off' and make rude gestures.

EMMA (laughing, too): And that wouldn't go so well!

When we meet two weeks later, Zoe tells me she has submitted the assignment she was worried about, and she's relatively pleased with it. A little internal freedom goes a long way.

Freedom from legacy burdens

Unburdening our parts liberates them, and when our parts are free, so are we. My session with Dick Schwartz was a remarkable demonstration of the liberation that comes when our parts break free from their burdens. At this point, we've received consent from several protective parts to return our focus to the tearful part of me with whom we began. That part took the form of water, a great sea of sadness:

DICK: How do you feel toward the sadness?

EMMA: I still feel blocked.

DICK: See who's blocking now.

EMMA: It feels like an observer part that can't interact.

DICK: Ask what it's afraid would happen if it let you interact with the sadness.

EMMA: We'd all drown.

DICK: Yeah, so tell it we understand that fear, but we're going to ask the sad part not to overwhelm you so you can be with it but not *become* it. So, nobody is going to drown if the sadness agrees not to overwhelm. Before you get any closer, we'll ask it not to overwhelm, and if it agrees to, it won't.

EMMA: I get the sense it almost wants to overwhelm.

DICK: Yes, of course. If it agrees, it will be easier to heal it, as these other parts won't be so scared.

EMMA (grinning): Yeah.

As we've seen, parts often think they are more constrained than they are: protectors believe they have no choice but to use their current strategies, while exiles believe they can't help but overwhelm us with the vastness of their suffering. Here Dick informs my sad part that it can simply choose not to overwhelm me – a liberation that brings spontaneous delight.

Later in the session, my teary exile begins to realize that the burden she is carrying, the belief that 'I am broken', was never hers to begin with – it was a legacy she inherited from my family. In my mind's eye, this part and I see our father behind bars:

DICK: Yes, she's not broken.

EMMA: That's all my family could see. And my father's in the prison, not her. He can't see what I see and what you see.

DICK: That's right.

EMMA: Sad.

DICK: For him, right?

EMMA: Yes.

Dick checks up on the connection between me and the little one, offering her a chance to have my Self witness her experience:

DICK: Does she need to show you anything about the past?
EMMA: We're looking at the dad.
DICK: Is there something she wants you to know about him?
EMMA: Almost like it's *his* sad I feel.
DICK: Just ask if that's right.
EMMA: I think so.
DICK: Is she ready to unload it and let go of it, now that you're there to take care of her?
EMMA: Yes, she carried it for him. He can't handle it.

Often, we help our exiles give inherited burdens back to the family members from whom they came. But, in this case, my little one tells Dick our father couldn't bear the burden if we did:

DICK: We won't give it to him, we'll just send it off.
EMMA: She'd like that ...
DICK: Is she and are you ready to let it go? Is there any fear about letting it go? ... Let her know that you're gonna be taking care of her now. She doesn't need him for that ... How would it feel now to send this out of your body?
EMMA: Good.
DICK: What would she like to give it up to?

You may recall what's happening here from **Chapter 6**. Dick is inviting my little one to give up her burden to an element which will destroy it, transform it, or carry it away. My exile chooses the element of air:

EMMA: Wind.
DICK: Out and off your body, let the wind carry it away.
EMMA (blowing air out of my mouth): Now we're doing light as well.

All of the burden is released to the air and the light. After a few more healing steps, my little one and I invite all my parts to gather round and welcome her into the here and now.

EMMA (smiling): She's waving.
DICK: How are they reacting?
EMMA: Curious.

DICK: Tell them to really check it out ... They can all think about new roles. The one who wants to make you laugh can start doing that.
EMMA: The one that kept all the bad stuff out can start letting the good stuff in.
DICK: Exactly, like love.

Freedom from cultural burdens

Lara Baden-Semper, whose presentation on ableism I've been sharing with you, explains how the burdens of internalized oppression operate outside of conscious awareness, and can be passed on from generation to generation. IFS helps us become aware of the oppression our parts have taken on so we can help them break free.

Cultural burdens, passed on through our families, often operate quite subtly. Lara offers an example of how her system's internalized cultural burdens, maintained through generations of family, affect how she responds to her son, whose ADHD and autistic characteristics (AuDHD for short) make it difficult for him to get ready on time in the morning. Her anxious parts, rageful parts and impatient parts use strategies of shaming, almost trying to bully her son out of behaviours driven by his particular nervous system – a style of neurodivergence Lara shares herself. Lara recognizes that she is responding to her son in much the same way her mother would have responded to her, and probably the same way her grandparents would have responded to her mother.

Fortunately, Lara was able to bring Self-energy to the parts of herself who were perpetuating an ableist reaction to her son.

- She helped her system get clear that, like her son, she was also neurodivergent.
- She freed her parts from using strategies derived from living in an ableist culture against her own parts and her son's.
- She created gentler and more effective ways of being with her own system and that of her son.

In fact, Lara credits the freedom IFS brought to her system with saving her relationship with her son, freeing both of them from the oppression of cultural burdens, and helping them both let go of the need to mask their neurodivergence – so they can connect authentically with each other and the world. Lara tells me that she has been able to get to and heal the wounds beneath the internalized ableist messages; she is liberated to show up as 'me'. If Lara can be free in this way, you and I can, too.

Freedom inside, freedom outside

Lara and I are both therapists, and as part of the job there is an implicit expectation that we attend to our own inner freedom. We don't often talk about this out loud, but perhaps we should – not least because we need inner freedom to assist others in breaking free from inner constraints, should they wish to. When therapists are free inside, we can show up authentically with our clients as we truly are – which can generate a virtuous cycle of unmasking, connecting with ourselves and with others in community and finding common cause.

Like Lara and me, your system may have internalized oppressive beliefs from the cultural waters in which we swim. We may house exiled parts who are burdened with painful core beliefs: *I'm stupid, broken, worthless, inferior* ... But it does not end there, Lara reminds us. She expressed the hope for freedom beautifully in a message I treasure: 'As we unshackle from the constraints of normativity, we reconnect with our essential energy. As we co-create our unique ways of being we challenge and change the world around us.'

My parts like to summarize, so here's a summary regarding freedom:

- Parts have the freedom to give space for Self to come to the fore.
- Parts respond well to having the freedom to say 'No, stop' and 'Yes, go ahead.' Exercising the power of choice is liberating.
- Parts have the freedom to reduce their intensity so as not to overwhelm or obscure Self.

- Parts carrying burdens (personal, legacy and cultural) can become free of them.
- Protectors become free to change roles once the exiles they protect are liberated.

Journal prompt

Exploring truth and freedom

- Can you get curious about your relationship to the truths about you? Below are some prompts. If you have old diaries or photos, they might serve as clues to inform your answers:
  - What truths about yourself, others and life did you hold as a child and young person?
  - Do you have a sense of where these truths came from?
  - How did these truths change in young adulthood if they did?
  - What are the truths you live by now if they are different?
  - Are any of those truths painful or limiting in some way?
  - Who in your inner world needs curious, loving attention and a listening ear?
  - Does someone inside seem to require the support of an IFS professional?

- Updating parts is a way of informing them that the burdensome truths they believe in are off, out of date or untrue in some way. Are there any liberating updates you can share with your parts right now?
- Are you aware of any of your nearest and dearest, or others in your circle who are carrying partial truths that are constraining their freedom? If so, can you get curious, clear and compassionate about how you might respond to that (if at all)?
- What does 'freedom' mean for you? How does it feature in your life? As you reflect, do you notice any reactions inside you or without? Can you respond to your reactions as trailheads or signposts worthy of exploration?

12

Emotional regulation and decreased reactivity

If you have been reading in a linear fashion and engaging with the journal prompts, you may already have noticed some welcome shifts in your ability to manage strong emotions internally and respond calmly to external others. These are common benefits of the therapeutic journey – life-changing blessings psychotherapists refer to somewhat clinically as 'emotional regulation' and 'decreased reactivity'.

Emotional regulation

Emotional regulation refers to our ability to manage our emotional experiences by reducing their intensity or adjusting how we respond to how we are feeling. Such regulation is a skill that can be acquired – metaphorically, a muscle that can be developed – which is fortunate, as many of us never learned how to do this as infants and children. For those of us who had a tough start in life, managing our emotions can be challenging. Without attuned attentiveness and bonding with 'good enough' caregivers at crucial stages of our development, we may struggle as adults to recognize, tolerate, soothe, or in other ways appropriately respond to our emotional experiences. Instead, our parts improvise ways to avoid, numb, stop or redirect our emotions.

Such strategies are protective, of course. In a system where parts dominate, protectors interpret intense emotions as crises to be managed with extreme behaviours of under- or over-regulation. I can certainly recognize my own protective system's emotion-control strategies, and perhaps you can, too – they have been known to use:

- avoidance
- crying uncontrollably
- **dissociating**
- impulsivity and reckless behaviour
- numbing
- raging
- self-injury
- mood-altering substances and behaviours, and even
- violent outbursts.

Such protective strategies often work well enough in a moment of overwhelming emotion. But they tend to lead to distressing consequences, which activate *other* overwhelming emotions, which start the whole cycle of protective reactivity all over. Parts with incompatible strategies for managing intense emotions often end up stuck in self-reinforcing polarizations that make us miserable, inside and out. In a Self-led system, our protective parts can stand down from the job of *controlling* our emotions so Self can help parts *regulate* them instead.

Dissociating

Dissociating means detaching from our experience in one way or another. It is often described as existing on a continuum. At one extreme, some people's systems have strongly compartmentalized parts who may not be aware of each other and don't share information, memories or experiences. On the milder end of the dissociative spectrum, many people's systems experience 'highway amnesia' – not recalling driving the route once you have arrived at a familiar destination. Across the continuum, IFS considers *dissociating* to be a natural, protective activity of parts.

I want to correct a common misimpression among some in IFS circles: regulating your emotions does *not* mean being perfectly and consistently calm, clear, compassionate, and otherwise exhibiting *only* the qualities of Self. Being able to emotionally regulate does not mean being permanently in some sort of 'Zen state' or having the inner psychic bus parked in neutral all the time. We could only achieve such inhuman serenity by being rid of our emotions altogether – the very opposite of what we're after if we are seeking emotional health and well-being.

Self-led emotional regulation happens when our parts feel confident enough in Self's leadership to feel the full range of their emotions, without trying to control or banish them – secure in the knowledge that they are not alone and unconditionally loved. So when a part is triggered and spikes extreme emotions within us, the system allows Self to come alongside the part that needs Self's compassionate presence and unconditional support. As our system trusts our Self to come alongside our parts, no matter how intense their feelings may be, spikes of overwhelming emotion become less intense organically.

Self helps our system regulate emotions in ways like these:

- welcoming parts with strong emotions *and* the parts reacting to them;
- having parts with concerns about emotions give space for Self to be with the part who's experiencing them;
- naming and validating parts' experiences exactly as they are;
- being curious towards a part who is experiencing extreme emotions;
- expressing or speaking for the emotions of a part or parts, internally or out loud;
- recognizing and meeting a part's needs, inside or in the external world;
- noticing and perhaps modifying environmental circumstances.

Once your Self is available to help parts with emotional regulation, your system might come to understand patterns of extreme feeling in helpful new ways. For example, by attending to inner and outer factors contributing to sharp emotional peaks and troughs, your system might decide to change your eating habits to flatten and lower your glucose curve.[1] Or your system might realize that a pattern of depression and anxiety has to do with the burdens an exiled part is bearing, and decide as a team to seek professional IFS support to help the little one unburden and heal.

Reactivity

You may recall how I described myself before I was tipped into a PTSD diagnosis and therapy: emotionless and 'in my head' most of the time. Well, back then I did sometimes get emotional – usually extremely so. This happened so rarely and so excessively that other people in my life were anything but understanding. One time, when I was tearfully confiding in my mother after a bad break-up, she suggested that my boyfriend ending our relationship was a good thing, despite my evident heartbreak. What I now recognize as a protective part sprang hotly to my defence, and I spoke harshly to her through my tears – a reaction my mother found so shocking she made an appointment for me to see a psychiatrist! At that time, I had little ability to manage my emotions; I was highly reactive. It was as if I lacked a fully functioning emotional skin or boundary: I could not manage or contain what I wanted to manage or contain (my distress at the end of the relationship), nor could I keep out what I wanted to keep out (my mother's thoughtless response).

The simplest example of emotional regulation I can think of is getting emotionally hurt by something, feeling and express-ing the hurt appropriately, and coming out the other side to a state of equanimity again. But, with a reactive system like mine used to be, there is a 'double whammy' effect when protectors try to control the initial hurt by shaming the parts who felt it.

I describe it to clients thus: the initial hurt occurs, and our parts then add extra layers of hurt in the form of harsh reactions, which we may well have learned from others: *I'm so weak, I should just get over it* or *No wonder he dumped me, I'm an emotional wreck.*

The Drama Triangle

You'll remember that parts energize parts and parts happen in patterns – some of which are particularly painful to experience and worth looking out for. One is the common polarization between an emotion-controlling firefighter and the long-suffering manager who has to clean up the mess the firefighter's strategies leave behind. Another pattern I notice frequently is familiar to me as a version of the Drama Triangle, sometimes known as 'Karpman's triangle', after its inventor (Karpman, 1968). In this configuration, a cluster of three parts play recognizable roles: the persecutor, the victim and the rescuer.[2] This pattern is common in systems I have come across living and working in England (including my own), where it seems these protective tendencies may be handed down across the generations to manage the true victimhood of so many, and the emotions that might arise if we were to grieve our suffering and the suffering the British Empire has inflicted on others.

Systems who have experienced many adverse childhood experiences (ACEs – see **Appendix 2**) often have wounded exiles around whom such a cluster of protectors constellates. The players in the Drama Triangle can do their work entirely within a person's system, but the pattern is more easily described between two people in the outside world. When a victim part is active in one person's system, parts in the other person's system react from one of the other corners, attempting either to persecute or to rescue the victim. Similarly, a rescuing part in me might 'recruit' a victim or persecutor part in you, and so on.

Each person can switch rapidly among the protectors involved, depending on who is in the driving seat of the two inner psychic buses.

These dynamics commonly appear in therapy, and it's worth being curious if you detect a Drama Triangle in your system or external relationships. This particular protective cluster tends to:

- prevent access to vulnerability inside (exiles are locked away and guarded ferociously);
- prevent access to internal Self-leadership (because the system is afraid the Self will get too close to the exiles);
- keep attention focused outside the system (through 'rescuing', shaming or desperately demanding help from others);
- maintain protective control at all costs.

The Drama Triangle is a tricky configuration, and you might benefit from some outside support if you find it in your system. An IFS professional can be effective in helping triangulated protectors agree to stepping aside for Self's healing presence to support them, as well as the exiles they protect. When clients' systems come to me in that configuration, I like to introduce an alternative to the Drama Triangle: the Healthy Triangle, in which a person can be healthily *vulnerable*, *responsive* to and *responsible* for their own emotions and emotional regulation, and *potent* or *powerful* in appropriate ways. These concepts are easily remembered, as they start with the same initial letter as the protective parts (v, r, p) – but they are not tidy substitutions, such that only 'victim' parts could become 'vulnerable', say. Rather, the Healthy Triangle describes ways of being in a Self-led system. It describes a relationship among parts in which *any* part's woundedness is met with responsiveness and appropriately powerful advocacy. Rather than being stuck in Drama Triangle reactivity, under Self's leadership, our parts can respond as their talents and the situation require.[3]

Taking things less personally

One of the staple benefits of any personal therapy or self-development activity is the decreased emotional reactivity that comes from learning that the upsetting situation isn't necessarily 'about me' at all. IFS is particularly helpful in this regard.

Here's an example shared by a client I'll call Regina. She and her wife, Manda, arranged to camp at the same site as Jay, an old flame of Regina's. The arrangements were otherwise loose; they were going to 'play it by ear'. In therapy, Regina's parts got clear about her wishes regarding the forthcoming meeting: to protect their primary relationship, safeguard the couple's time from doing things they didn't want to do, and making time to do some of what they did want to do. She's come back to therapy after the trip, seeming surprised and happy:

REGINA: We had a great time; the weather was just right so we got lots of walking in.

EMMA: That was good timing; you sound excited, too. I'm curious what you're excited about.

REGINA: Well, I realize I've not been in therapy with you for long, and I've had these self-esteem issues in the past.

EMMA: Sure.

REGINA: And we talked about how I was a bit concerned about the three of us meeting up, me and Manda plus my ex, Jay.

EMMA: I remember. We spent time with a protector and got a glimpse of an exile carrying feelings of rejection.

REGINA: Yes. Anyway, I'd forgotten how all-over-the-place Jay can be. It's one crisis after another with him. So, we spent time together on the first day and he said he'd be leaving the following day, but not until the middle of the afternoon, so the three of us would have time to visit this cool farm shop nearby.

EMMA: Okay, that sounds friendly.

REGINA: That's the thing – the way Jay was talking, I just knew it wasn't going to happen! It was so clear he was talking from a part. And I was curious, wondering what the other parts inside Jay were wanting about when to leave. Like, you could tell there was no inner consensus!

> EMMA: I can see some of why you're excited – this awareness about Jay's inner complexity seems a revelation for you.
>
> REGINA: Absolutely, and more to the point, I was wondering what crisis was going to appear and prevent this part's plan about visiting the shop anyway. Sure enough, the following day, Jay shows up after breakfast: 'Okay, I'm leaving in an hour, I've got to go at once, let's have one last coffee.'
>
> EMMA: Just as you'd predicted.
>
> REGINA: Yes, I wasn't surprised – and, more importantly, it didn't hurt like it would have done in the past.
>
> EMMA: Can you tell me more?
>
> REGINA: I was explaining it to Manda on the drive home – it's like no one on the inside took to heart what Jay's plan-making-part said the day before. It just felt so clear that Jay announcing a change of plan wasn't about us; it was about *Jay's* system and how *they* decide and react to stuff. We'd done nothing wrong.

In the past, Regina told me, parts in her would have taken Jay's change of plan personally, been swept into a turmoil of feeling rejected and confused (a victim protector perhaps), experiencing self-blame plus anger outwards (an inner and outer persecutor). A part of Regina would have sent messages to Jay wanting to educate him about how to better manage relationships and be more thoughtful (a rescuer perhaps, who would have been experienced by Jay as persecutory). Now that Regina is alert to parts in herself and others, there's more freedom from Drama Triangle dynamics. Her system realizes that Jay's plan-making and plan-cancelling parts are simply doing their best to protect him, just as Regina's parts do their best to protect her.

Getting comfortable with feelings

How has Regina arrived at this freedom from reactivity? In a variety of ways. She has taken to heart the message of multiplicity in others. She has chosen a mantra summing up the IFS concept of parts as having positive intentions which often proves useful: 'They are doing the best they can.' More importantly, she has become the primary caretaker for her inner family, communicating to all her parts that they matter to her and she's not about to reject them. As well as having a wife with whom she can share aspects of her inner world, her parts no longer need to recruit unreliable others like Jay to care for her **emotional pain.**

Of course, Regina's journey to this point has not been easy. Many of us experienced formative years in which our parts accumulated burdens of rejection, abandonment, feeling uncared-for and neglected. As a result, we learned to reject the most vulnerable parts of ourselves, to abandon and neglect the exiles within. In the past, Regina's protectors would have growled resentfully that *Jay shouldn't have made a promise he couldn't keep,* or blamed Regina for having been hurt by his change of plans: *You know what he's like, so why are you so upset?* Still others would have tried to save the day by making plans for Regina to manipulate Jay into better behaviour next time. It often results in protectors attempting to shut down emotions (both the awareness and the expression of them). They then accumulate under the surface where the pressure of unexpressed and unexperienced emotions builds and builds, becoming liable to explode uncontrollably as a means for the system to let off steam and bring about some regulation.

Feeling emotional pain

Parts can be convinced that the way to healing is through big experiences of emotion (screaming, crying, punching pillows). Such dramatic gestures really might be healing in the presence of Self, or a Self-led other who is fully present. Without Self's support, though, acting out our emotional pain has the potential to scare parts of us and others and keep things stuck. What heals is the you-who's-not-a-part being with, holding, containing and relating to parts in emotional pain. It's about being both *in* our feelings and *alongside* or *with them.*

Updating parts about emotions

A client I'll call Gloria is in her early fifties; she works full-time, her husband having died young, and she has recently become an empty nester. Having had some therapy before, she has come across IFS and it appeals to her. She tells me she has enjoyed drawing, collaging and choosing photos from magazines to represent her parts, and she's come to me for support 'getting to know my parts a bit better'. I have not made an enquiry into Gloria's history partly because she is so keen to share her progress with what she calls 'parts work' and partly because I have a sense to tread very gently, at her system's pace. I am also aware that 'getting to know parts a bit better' may have a subtext that is yet to be revealed.

Gloria and I meet online, and our early sessions involve her introducing me to many members of her inner family. I welcome each one, enquiring about internal relationships and roles, and generally flexing my curiosity muscles – both head and heart. It becomes apparent that one of the reasons Gloria chose to represent her parts externally with drawings and pictures is because the sheer number of them feels overwhelming – it is 'noisy' inside. I quickly learn about the existence of various polarities among the members of Gloria's team:

- One says, *Find a man now you're home alone*, while another urges her to *Enjoy the solitude, this is time for you now.*
- Another mourns, *I can't stop crying on the sofa now my babies have flown the nest*, while someone else says cheerfully, *At last, I can do all those extra jobs I've had no time for.*

Gloria has some curiosity available, in sessions and out, which she follows by asking her protectors to 'dial it back' and not overwhelm the system with their loud disagreements with each other. 'Whenever I notice a part or a few parts,' she tells me, 'I thank them for showing up and suggest that if they would like to communicate with me, it works best one at a time because, "If you rush at me all at once, I can't hear you or really be here anymore." That seems to quieten them down; it's almost as if they are shocked someone's there and wants to listen. If any of them then want to talk and the timing's right, we do, and I can jot notes down on my phone. Or, if it's inconvenient, I arrange to listen later when I bring out the pictures of my parts.'

Gradually, without my pushing, Gloria's parts are beginning to tell her more about their stories, and as they do she starts to share her thoughts with me about her early start in life:

GLORIA: When I was five, my parents split up, and my stepfather arrived with twin girls a year older than me. They were perfect, and I couldn't do a thing right in his eyes or theirs. They were always down on me; Mother just let them gang up on me. That's what it felt like anyway.
EMMA: Do you have a sense of who that affected inside?
GLORIA: I used to feel so terrible, torn between wanting to hide and wanting to be part of this new family somehow. I hid it all, of course, no one wanted to know how I felt.
EMMA: It sounds like when you were little your feelings were made to be 'wrong' and not welcomed. Am I understanding some of how it was for you back then? (Gloria nods gently.) I'm wondering if that's why you showing an interest in your parts now feels so positive.
GLORIA: Yes, although I wish I didn't feel so anxious all the time. Other women my age don't fall apart like I keep doing.

Here we glimpse a protector who is anti-emotion – judging the crying on the sofa as 'falling apart'.

EMMA: It's quite understandable that a part of you feels distress at the loss you are experiencing in the present, which seems to be linking up with past losses you may or may not have grieved back then.
GLORIA: Perhaps.
EMMA: It makes sense you have a part who feels anxious and on edge a lot of the time; perhaps it worries that the part holding the sadness might take over inside. Can you point the anxious one out to me in your album?
GLORIA: Yes, that makes sense; it's him.

Gloria smiles very slightly as she points to the image of a businesslike manager at a computer, whom she's described previously as super-hot on productivity and *keeping on keeping on*.

> EMMA: How does it feel to link that anxiety with this part?
> GLORIA: A relief. Like I feel bigger than he is right now.
> EMMA: Sure. How do you feel towards him?
> GLORIA: Welcoming and open.

I invite Gloria to share this openness and welcome with the part. She closes her eyes and senses inside.

> GLORIA: He's kind of stopped what he's doing with his spreadsheets and noticed me. He's not sure who I am.
> EMMA: Is he curious, do you sense?
> GLORIA (nodding, with her hand gently resting on his image): Yes, he is.
> EMMA: Great, see if you can update him about who you are. Or, I am happy to talk with him directly, if you and he prefer that.
> GLORIA: Yes, you do it. He's looking between the two of us a bit confused, but he heard you suggest that, and he nodded.
> EMMA: Okay, thank you. (I address the part.) Hello, you are welcome! I'm glad to meet you and have this opportunity to introduce you and Gloria to each other. Gloria is in therapy with me to get to know you and other parts inside. Do you know Gloria? ... (No response, so I try again.) Just off the top of your head, do you know how old Gloria is?
> SPREADSHEET PART: Primary school age, little, I ...

The part seems confused, even startled slightly, which I acknowledge.

> EMMA: Yes, it can be a bit confusing; time has moved on, and Gloria is now in her fifties with grown children. While you and other parts have been stuck at certain ages, life also carried on. How old do you think you are?
> SPREADSHEET PART: I'm young, too. I'm in charge. (Gloria is holding herself upright – it's as if the part is communicating a sense of pride in itself. Then her body sags slightly.) But it's hard. She's so unhappy and alone. I try and make her feel better by staying very active and on top of stuff.

EMMA: Yes, you do a great job of that. I'm sure Gloria appreciates that. Meanwhile, can I highlight that the Gloria who is so unhappy and alone is another part of her, like you; whereas there is a Gloria-who's-not-a-part who would like to get to know you and help you and the sad lonely one.

SPREADSHEET PART: I hadn't realized. I feel bad I didn't know that. I'm supposed to manage things.

EMMA: Sure, I understand it's confusing. You really haven't done anything wrong. You've been trying to prevent the system from being flooded by emotions that grind it to a halt, yes?

Gloria seems slightly more upright, as if the part has perked up; I can almost imagine him puffing out his chest.

SPREADSHEET PART: I have been trying to do that. And blocking emotions that used to get her attacked, called names and sent to her room.

EMMA: That sounds hard for you both. The Gloria-who-isn't-a-part is also not like those people who couldn't tolerate little Gloria's emotions.

SPREADSHEET PART: She's not?

EMMA: No, and with your permission, she can be with the part feeling alone and unhappy, and in time help it.

SPREADSHEET PART: Then things will be easier for me, I guess. Is it Gloria who's been telling parts to go one at a time? That's been useful.

EMMA: That's right! In the longer term we'd like to make life easier for you. But first, would you like to meet Gloria directly? Not that I don't want to keep talking with you. If it's okay with you, I'll stay here with you both.

SPREADSHEET PART: Okay sure, what do I have to do?

EMMA: Well, I'm not sure exactly, you'll find your own way to make space inside for the Gloria-who's-not-a-part. Somehow relax control a little – for now – so Gloria can come and be with you and get to know you.

And he does! Gloria spends time in and outside sessions being with and welcoming this hardworking manager. In time he gives Gloria and me permission to approach the sad and lonely exile whose emotions he has been protecting the system from. This little one is delighted to meet Gloria – someone who cares about her and how she feels and what she's been through. This little one asked for more comfort, which Gloria gladly provided by giving her an imaginary blanket and her favourite story-books. Gloria checks in with her regularly.

As we continue with 'parts work', I have been updating her parts about the function and role of emotions. For example:

- Emotions are normal. Humans create them in our bodies, and they are designed to flow through us – not be ignored, squashed down, diverted or attacked.
- If allowed and enabled to flow, emotions generally have a lifecycle all their own and naturally come and go.
- Parts holding emotions, comfortable and uncomfortable ones alike, have important information for us: *I'm angry because* ... ; *I'm afraid because* ... ; *I feel relief when* ....
- It's understandable that parts take on beliefs from family or society such as: *If I cry it means something is wrong with me* or *Big girls don't cry* or *Anger isn't safe.* We take on those beliefs because they helped us stay safe when we were small.
- But beliefs can transform, and behaviours can be changed that no longer serve the system.

The more her parts learn about how emotions really work, the more curious they get, and Gloria does quite a bit of self-directed reading. As her parts start to feel more comfortable with their feelings, they let Gloria make some positive changes in her everyday life. She makes sure she has regular contact with her grown children and, especially with her youngest daughter, she risks showing some emotion (or at least speaking *for* it) at times. That feels scary at first, but her parts notice that the world keeps on turning. Gloria notices that her levels of what she used to call 'self-pity' and 'self-loathing' have dropped dramatically; her parts get to feel their feelings without shame, secure in the knowledge that Gloria loves them just as they are.

Speaking for our needs and negotiating for change

Emotional regulation is primarily an 'inside job', achieved when parts trust Self as their primary caretaker and leader. But the outside world can contribute too. Here is a personal example between me and my husband. One of our first holidays as a married couple was a trip to Europe by train. It began badly; we ended up running down the hill to the train station towing our wheelie luggage, and we missed the train! That wasn't our last stressful top-speed dash for a train, and the next time it happened I was seriously concerned at how much stress it put on my body and my breathing. It also fuelled negative emotions towards and judgements of my *tardy, disorganized* and *inconsiderate* husband, not least because my managers keep to certain principles: *be early; prepare ahead of time; do not keep anyone waiting, it's rude.* Arriving late to the train station made my parts suspect that I simply didn't matter to my husband – *unwanted, uncared-for, unloved.*

What to do about it? Ahead of an upcoming trip, I got curious about my husband's perception of our differing approaches to time and travel; I also invited his curiosity towards my system. Thankfully, he was interested in how his approach impacted my parts and the messages they perceived, which allowed my protectors to be less judgemental towards him. He did not want to contribute in this way to my system's sense of not mattering, but explained that he struggles with being *early* – his system is uncomfortable with transitions and 'hanging around'. In collaboration, we got curious: Was there a way for both our systems to have their needs met and make the train?

It turns out the answer is yes: if it's a local jaunt, I set off under my own steam to the train station, buy the tickets and enjoy mooching around and being early. My husband then enjoys dashing up the hill to arrive on the platform just as the train pulls into the station. If it's a longer journey involving lots of luggage – my husband's parts like to travel heavy; mine like to travel light – then he drives me and all the luggage up to the train station and drops us off early. I wait there while he zips home, does whatever he feels still needs to be done, leaves the car at home, then hustles up the hill to join us.

I think for some of us, women especially, it takes courage to speak for our needs, for our tenderest parts, who grew up not feeling worthy of asking someone else to adapt to meet those needs. Self-leadership makes the difference. My husband and I both still have our own inner struggles, of course, but leaving to go on holiday is certainly less stressful *between us*.

Journal prompt

Your evolving emotional experience

- As you look back over your life since you began reading and engaging with this book, do you notice any shifts in your emotional landscape?
- Do you recall anyone making a comment about how you seem different in a way that relates to your emotions or reactivity?
- If it feels right, using the prompts in the second column of the table below, ask yourself what you notice about your emotions recently.
- List what you are aware of in the third column or in your journal if you keep one. You could even get curious about your emotional landscape on a regular basis from now on.

Emotions	Prompts	Current awareness
Joy Sadness Fear Anger Surprise Disgust Pride Shame Embarrassment Excitement *Add others relevant to you.*	Moving through more quickly Arising with less fear Feeling more acceptable More noticeable than before Less intense Enjoying feeling them Or maybe it is hard to notice any changes.	

13

Self-acceptance and authenticity

Authenticity seems to be a much-used word in modern Western society, though it seems not to be uniformly understood. Culturally, 'being authentic' is presented as a 'must' – as an aspirational goal to attain. For some it means something like integrity: 'walking the talk' and striving to align your actions with core beliefs and values. That kind of authenticity often requires change. Other times, it means staying 'true to your roots' – perhaps by keeping your regional accent rather than succumbing to pressures to speak what used to be revered as 'the Queen's English'. That version of authenticity is about *not* changing.

To be thought authentic, a psychotherapist like me must be genuine and caring, have a way of being down-to-earth, 'real', not simply acting a part. Meanwhile, clients often come to therapy with the desire to become more authentic themselves, bringing vague but alluring notions of 'being oneself', 'not violating one's own self-concept' and striving to arrive at 'the true self'.

For those who are comfortable in their self-understanding and presentation, authenticity may not be something they have given much time to considering. I am not one of those people! As a twin who grew up in the 1960s and 1970s, when twins seemed rarer than they are these days, authenticity was inevitably going to become a 'thing' for me. The challenges of your life might have given you reasons to ponder authenticity and identity for yourself. Nic Wildes, a transmasculine mental health counsellor from the USA, observes that we only worry about being authentic when difficulties challenge our sense of self: 'Folks who are not experiencing any hardship don't often think to ask these kinds of questions' (2023, p. 147).

Reconsidering authenticity

So far as I can tell, there is some common ground among those who use and value the idea of authenticity. Being authentic takes effort, requires courage, and is a good thing. But as an IFS professional, my parts who are dyed-in-the-wool champions of multiplicity (and openly pedantic regarding the meanings and uses of words) are vexed that people persist in understanding the self who is authentic or not as *just one thing*. I agree with marketing specialist Lara Eastburn of One Word: 'When I hear folks say, "Just be yourself," my go-to response tends to be "Ummm. Which *one*?"'[1]

It is understandable that, in an individualistic culture, 'authenticity' is widely understood in a radically singular way. When people talk about someone's being 'inauthentic' – meaning 'phony' and 'fake' – the implication is that their complexity is a vice; nobody ought to be 'two-faced'. IFS gives us a much more nuanced and realistic understanding of people's complexity. We all have parts who are other than they seem. Different protectors may well interface with the outside world in ways that make us seem quite inconsistent. A part that feels it must dominate the inner system will regularly pose as a singular self, without complexity – which leads to bewildering inconsistencies, since other parts will inevitably insist on making themselves known. Being 'authentic' in the sense of *singular* is simply unrealistic, at least with an IFS understanding of what's real.

For me, authenticity is not about returning to or finding a singular ideal 'true self'. That would be to banish treasured inner family members and hamper a person's ability to navigate life. In an IFS sense, I consider that being authentic means honouring *all* of who we are – Self and parts with their gifts and burdens, hopes, dreams and nightmares, and a body, too. Our parts are what make us unique! Let's not try and 'integrate them away' in the chase for a supposedly unified 'true self'.

Remember, we take it as given that our parts are inherent: they don't 'arrive' or 'develop' through 'splitting' or 'fragmenting'. They step up to serve their system at specific points in time and in certain contexts – to protect, carry burdens or offer their gifts. Parts deserve to be in harmonious and balanced relationships inside with a Self who leads and loves them. That way we can live in harmony and balance in external relationships and support others in *their* complex authenticity. For me, how a person thinks about authenticity directly links to self-acceptance. If we are striving to reduce our inner world to a singular 'true self', we cannot offer welcome and acceptance to all of who we are. Is it not a part doing the striving?

Self-acceptance: finding your tribe

I have learned much from Nic Wildes about authenticity and self-acceptance. They write about the benefits of community and the 'particular kind of ease' they feel among a group of people with shared identity, understanding and experiences. In such an **affinity group**, our parts can feel less shame and relax their 'fierce protection'. We all need places, spaces and groups that welcome *all* of who we are with open arms, where we see our systems reflected by and in others.

> **Affinity groups**
> Places created so that marginalized people with shared identities can come together with less fear and more affirmation. (Adapted from Foot and Redfern, 2023, p. 267)

Naturally, it is not as easy as it sounds. Nic had to address internalized transphobia and befriend the parts inside who were so reactive to them being trans. That took commitment and dedication on the inside and outside, and community was key. A tough protector, who shielded Nic from emotions, found truth and freedom in fellowship with other queer people:

> Truly, it was being in community that helped my tough guy begin to soften and begin to trust that it would be okay to soften. ... with connection to community as an anchor and a resource of Self-energy, he and the team have begun to trust that, even when not in community and affinity spaces, I have the courage and confidence to stand tall. (Wildes 2023, pp. 148–9)

Personally and professionally, Nic's system now provides such spaces for others.

Trans or not, we all benefit from finding our tribes. Helen Foot, a certified IFS practitioner and project management professional with a master's in social work in New Zealand, sees reflections of her own system in others who work in the health and social services field:

> I saw how I could bring IFS to these people with systems always giving, not seeking therapy, or who might see therapy as 'fluffy stuff' irrelevant in their technical work environment. This is my stomping ground, it fits, I understand the drive and parts of leaders that need to be competent no matter what. This became my IFS client group, the people I support ... (Foot, 2023, p. 30)

Accepting *all* of who we are

Although IFS posits that multiplicity is natural, it also understands that there is a strong cultural tendency towards monomindedness – a cultural burden some parts of us naturally take on. Parts who are uncomfortable with parts are welcome too! Ash Chudgar, an IFS coach in the USA, writes (in late 2024) that 'ambivalence is healthy and good':

In our minds as in our external communities, vigorous dissent is democratic; being consistently 'of one mind' is a warning sign of inner autocracy. ... Your ambivalence shows that you're *human*. Welcome to your own plurality! It's a trip!

If there's one thing I know for certain, it's that accepting and even *valuing* the diversity of perspectives within yourself – not choosing sides, not censoring any thought or wish, not shaming any part of who you are for thinking any thought – will make you much more comfortable as you navigate the complexities of human life. And as history complicates our lives faster and more completely than we could possibly predict, our plurality can save us – not just from emotional discomfort, but from the harmful seduction of enforced consensus. White supremacy, ethno-nationalism, nativism – these totalitarian ideologies attract the parts of people who are frightened by the mere fact of diversity. Honoring our own internal diversity is the most potent anti-fascist action we can take.

So lean into your bonkers ambivalence, friends! I promise you'll feel better if you do. ... That is the substance of this plural tip: *we are all diverse*, all the way down. Nobody is just one thing; to be human is to be multiple. And that knowledge, all by itself, can help you stay sane in these unprecedented times.

Finding a balance

In modern Western society, in my personal and professional experience, women are expected to *be all things to all people*. We keep multiple plates spinning and 'service' multiple relationships. Secretly we may want to *have it all* (or feel we must) – and yet women also often feel silently guilty about wanting more than one thing and engender feelings of failure when 'it all' gets too much. In her autobiography, Michelle Obama writes of recognizing a desire to be 'both a Mary and a Marian' (2018, p. 174). Like so many modern Western women, Michelle was caught in an unsolvable riddle – as IFS would call it, a polarization between parts with opposing strategies. Michelle finds herself caught between wanting to be a free-spirited independent career woman like Mary Tyler Moore and wanting to be like her selfless stay-at-home mother, Marian, who gave diligently and in full to her family. Such internal conflicts are common among women, and IFS gives us a powerful way to find balance in them.

A talented and dear friend of mine in her sixties works and lives alone very happily, though she shares her life with an intimate partner too. She told me she is due to be hosting her adult child and their partner for a time, and has concerns about signs of her professional life remaining on show in communal areas. 'I don't want my daughter to feel I'm not her mother,' a concerned part of my friend tells me. We explore how she can be *both* her daughter's loving mother *and* a successful professional. These identities are not mutually exclusive: one need not detract from the other. Yet, attention to balance is needed. We all only have 24 hours per day and one lifespan, and depending on our mental and physical health, resources, geography, demands upon us, and so forth, we only have so much energy. Our parts can be who they are, but we cannot live out all their dreams.

Paradoxically, accepting the constraints of our circumstances can help our parts feel much more free. Lara Baden-Semper, whom I introduced in an earlier chapter, has found self-acceptance through letting go of the norms of Western society around 'wellness'. She urges that we tend to and check in on any of our parts who believe a certain ideal of wellness is something we should all strive for. Instead, she encourages us to value the sharing of our own differences and different identities, as well as the embracing and modelling of our human variability. She communicated to me that 'unpacking our internalized ableism frees us to hold space for the infinite ways in which we can find a way to be ourselves'.

In conclusion

I recently saw a social-media post suggesting that one's life story can be written in six words. *Enticing!* thought a writerly part of me, who came up with this: 'Fear froze; therapy thawed; showing up.' What six words would you choose today to describe your life story?

As I come to the end of my journey with you, I remind myself of my intentions for this book and for you: that it both satisfies and piques your curiosity about Internal Family Systems; that it encourages you to use elements of it and, when appropriate, to seek support from a professional trained in IFS. I hope that you might have come to know and love the parts of yourself more fully, widely and deeply. May your inner journey always be in progress; I assure you there is still time. May you show up more fully, with less need to hide yourself or parts of yourself. May you have places and relationships where hiding feels less crucial and necessary for survival and comfort. May you never stop getting curious, inside and out.

Journal prompt

Welcoming all, banishing none

What does authenticity mean to you? Perhaps your search for authenticity is a lifelong journey, or perhaps it is a reclaiming of exiled parts of yourself into a harmonious, accepting, and welcoming system?

Here is a quotation from the core textbook of IFS. As you read it, be curious and notice who responds inside and how:

> Self-acceptance is the ongoing process of welcoming all parts and banishing none. When we pursue the ideal of self-acceptance we also gain the freedom to live by curiosity, exploration, and inclusion. (Schwartz and Sweezy, 2020, p. 42)

Can you pay attention to any constraints or blocks to the idea of self-acceptance? Is it possible to think of these as trailheads or signposts leading you to a part (or parts) to welcome with your warm, open-hearted curiosity?

Section 6
MORE TO EXPLORE

Appendix 1
A Self-leadership measure

Self-leadership refers to your capacity to be open-heartedly curious and compassionate towards every part of who you are. When you are Self-led, the you-who's-not-a-part can hear from, validate, acknowledge and appreciate your parts for their service in your system and in the world. I've created a brief check-in quiz to help you get a snapshot of your Self-leadership at a certain time.[1]

In the first column of the answers to the first statement, you'll put the date of your check-in – I'd suggest trying now, then perhaps six months later, and then six months after that. But the column is blank so you can choose your preferred timescales.

For each statement, put a tick mark in the box that seems accurate to you. To register improvement or otherwise, compare the placement of ticks at the different timeframes; you will be able to see if they are moving in the direction you are hoping for.

1. My parts feel appreciated.

Date	Frequently	Often	Sometimes	Seldom	Almost never

2. I believe all my parts have positive intentions.

Date	Frequently	Often	Sometimes	Seldom	Almost never

3. I can listen to and calm inner conflict.

Date	Frequently	Often	Sometimes	Seldom	Almost never

4. I feel alone.

Date	Frequently	Often	Sometimes	Seldom	Almost never

5. I can be present to and soothe inner distress.

Date	Frequently	Often	Sometimes	Seldom	Almost never

6. My parts offer their ideas and opinions without hijacking my system.

Date	Frequently	Often	Sometimes	Seldom	Almost never

7. I like being me.

Date	Frequently	Often	Sometimes	Seldom	Almost never

8. I feel compelled to do extreme things that feel problematic.

Date	Frequently	Often	Sometimes	Seldom	Almost never

9. I am confident about who I am; I don't rely on others' judgements.

Date	Frequently	Often	Sometimes	Seldom	Almost never

10. I can be curious inside.

Date	Frequently	Often	Sometimes	Seldom	Almost never

11. I enjoy being creative.

Date	Frequently	Often	Sometimes	Seldom	Almost never

12. My parts give space inside for me to be with them.

Date	Frequently	Often	Sometimes	Seldom	Almost never

13. My parts take over and it's a problem.

Date	Frequently	Often	Sometimes	Seldom	Almost never

14. My system experiences inner freedom.

Date	Frequently	Often	Sometimes	Seldom	Almost never

15. I feel on guard and defended.

Date	Frequently	Often	Sometimes	Seldom	Almost never

16. I have psychological and emotional flexibility.

Date	Frequently	Often	Sometimes	Seldom	Almost never

17. My parts take over and it's not a problem.

Date	Frequently	Often	Sometimes	Seldom	Almost never

18. It feels easy to make decisions.

Date	Frequently	Often	Sometimes	Seldom	Almost never

19. I feel able to meet life's challenges.

Date	Frequently	Often	Sometimes	Seldom	Almost never

20. I use criticism and judgement.

Date	Frequently	Often	Sometimes	Seldom	Almost never

21. I feel peaceful and spacious inside.

Date	Frequently	Often	Sometimes	Seldom	Almost never

22. I can speak *for* my parts rather than *from* them.

Date	Frequently	Often	Sometimes	Seldom	Almost never

23. My parts give me space to attend to them and to external others simultaneously.

Date	Frequently	Often	Sometimes	Seldom	Almost never

Use this extra space to list additional statements of your choice that indicate your Self-leadership, and how often you experience them:

_____

_____

Date	Frequently	Often	Sometimes	Seldom	Almost never

_____

_____

Date	Frequently	Often	Sometimes	Seldom	Almost never

_____

_____

Date	Frequently	Often	Sometimes	Seldom	Almost never

Appendix 2
Adverse childhood experiences and protective factors

Adverse childhood experiences

Adverse childhood experiences (ACEs) are traumatic events we experience under the age of 18 without the aid of a loving, Self-led other to help us respond to them. These experiences can have long-term impacts on our health, well-being and life opportunities. From an IFS perspective our parts help us survive adverse experiences we encounter in childhood by taking on the jobs they do to keep overwhelming feelings away and protect us to the best of their abilities.

Here are some examples of ACEs – some you might have encountered growing up, others you managed to escape. As you consider them, you might get curious about how a child's parts might respond to help them survive:

- Having a family member with acute emotional or physical needs
- Living in poverty
- Being bullied at school
- Being **abused** or exploited in any way (emotional, psychological, physical, racial, sexual)
- Experiencing or witnessing domestic violence
- Being ridiculed or shamed for being different from peers or family members
- Living in foster care
- Living in or fleeing a war zone or place of danger
- Living through or fleeing a natural disaster
- Losing of a family member to suicide

- Losing a parent or caregiver through divorce, death or abandonment
- Being seriously ill or hospitalized
- Having a relative imprisoned
- Being neglected by parents or caregivers (emotional, psychological, physical)
- Having family members with untreated mental illness or addiction
- Premature or traumatic birth.

Abuse

The term for the unfair use of physical, psychological or social power against others who are unable to defend themselves effectively because they do not have equal physical, psychological or social power.

ACEs aren't a child's fault – nor are the ways their parts respond to help them survive as best they can. Tragically, children often undergo ACEs because the adults in their lives are acting from burdened parts of their own – parts who might well have taken on *their* extreme roles in similar childhood circumstances. To be clear: we can have compassion for every part of everyone without condoning any behaviour that results in a child being harmed. Accountability and responsibility are important, but this is a very complex subject. Bringing compassion and curiosity to it will be useful.

The Manchester NHS Foundation Trust website cites a 2014 study which indicates that, in the UK, 47 per cent of people experienced at least one ACE with 9 per cent of the population having four or more ACES (Bellis et al., 2014).[1]

Effects of ACEs on physical and mental health

It is becoming more widely accepted that the longer a person experiences an ACE, and the more ACEs they experience, the greater the risk to their long-term well-being. ACEs predispose people to certain health problems in adulthood, such as cancer and heart disease, as well as increasing the risk of mental health difficulties. According to Manchester University NHS Foundation Trust, one in three diagnosed mental health conditions in adulthood directly relate to adverse childhood experiences.

But there is good news! Even if you have experienced many ACEs, there is hope through transformational therapies such as Internal Family Systems. Preventing ACEs and mitigating their effects through supportive relationships and environments can significantly improve health outcomes and reduce the impact of these experiences.

Protective factors and prevention

Protective factors are experiences that may decrease the risks that come from ACEs. As you read these examples, I'd encourage you to get curious about how these positive experiences might help someone's parts (perhaps your own) develop in strong, unburdened ways:

- Having a positive experience of schooling
- A predictable home routine, like regular meals and a regular bedtime
- A significant relationship with someone you now recognize as Self-led and able to access Self-energy
- Knowing an adult outside of the home who can provide support, advice, or caring
- At least one caregiver with whom you feel safe
- At least one good friend who feels supportive

- At least one teacher who cares about you
- Beliefs that give you comfort
- Caregivers with access to resources (financial, medical, community, etc.)
- Feeling good in your body and enjoying your physical abilities
- Friendly neighbours or community support
- Opportunities for fun and play
- Participation in family or community activities and traditions
- Positive feelings towards yourself or feeling comfortable with yourself.

Supporting children from Self

It is beyond the scope of this book to address supporting children's systems in depth. However, in line with the ethos of this book, here are some ideas for helping young people in your life cope with any adversity they may experience:

- Share the concept of parts and Self with children in ways they can understand. Notice when Self qualities are available in you and in children as resources.[2]
- When a part leads your system with negative consequences for young people, take responsibility and apologize to the child for any hurt your part caused them. Inside, forgive your part for having got it wrong this time; children are resilient. Grant your system the chance to start over with inner compassion and creativity.
- Communication is key. Talk and listen to young people and provide whatever support they are willing to accept, and you have the resources to provide. The very act of communicating – including listening, showing you've heard, and speaking – persistently over time signals you care. The caring of even one Self-led adult is a powerful protective factor in any child's life.

- At times of increased stress in the family, such as bereavement, illness, relocation or financial hardships, children and young people may feel less able or less willing to communicate about how they are feeling with family members. At such times, it is even more important to attend to communication, even if you can't provide it yourself. You can consider introducing children to peer groups that are overseen in some way, where they might feel freer to talk about their experiences.

- Watch for signs of distress in children and young people, such as an increase in firefighter behaviours (anger, upped intake of TV or games, sleeping less or more, self-isolation, and the like), and a reduction in manager behaviours (doing less well at school or being uncharacteristically late, for example). Seek professional help, if you can, when you feel it's needed.

- Lean on support from Self on the inside and from Self-led others outside. Find ways to let your parts do and be what they enjoy, as well as what they 'must' and 'should'. The more harmonious your system is, the more Self-energy you will be able to bring to the little ones in your life.

Appendix 3
To be (or not to be) in IFS therapy

When it might be a good idea to seek therapy

You don't have to work with an IFS professional to put the model into practice for yourself – indeed, I've written this book primarily with do-it-yourselfers in mind. But as I've written many times, it is sometimes very helpful to seek out a professional to help you work with your parts.

Not all IFS professionals are therapists like me; many are trained in other forms of mental health care, like social work or psychiatry, and some are non-clinical practitioners who work as coaches or consultants. But every sort of IFS professional can help you do therapeutic work, so I'll call it 'therapy' for short.

You might want to seek IFS therapy:

- as you begin to learn about the model and want to familiarize yourself with the Fs, Cs, processes and patterns;
- to do healing work with your exiles, especially if they persistently overwhelm the you-who's-not-a-part, neutralizing your curiosity;
- when dangerous firefighters are frightening parts in your system or in others' systems, and potentially endangering life and limb;
- if your system has strong boundaries between parts resulting in signs of dissociation – for example, losing time, regularly 'coming to' somewhere with no knowledge of how you got there or what happened before, feeling 'switches' that cause you concern or distress, or feeling that life is unreal;
- when you and your partner are struggling together;
- when you have felt stuck or hopeless for a while;
- for companionship and support over the long haul.

For a focused piece of inner work – at a time of transition, for example, or to help a particularly dominant protector relax.

Therapy is not necessarily going to be easy

Deep inner work isn't always a good idea. If your life circumstances are unsafe or volatile, or are likely to change drastically, it might not be a good time to delve deeply into your inner world. Giving your protective parts the resources they need in the present might be more appropriate for now.

If you do decide to pursue therapy, go into it with your eyes open:

- It can feel like things get worse before they get better.
- Perhaps therapy brings freedom to unmask, to speak out, to make or expect changes that impact your outer world and those in it.
- When one system changes through self-development, the systems of other people in your life may feel threatened. Protectors may polarize across systems or attempt to bolster the status quo.
- What seemed 'fine' previously may now appear differently, perhaps worse. You might see your childhood in a new and darker light, or discover you aren't as satisfied with a current partner.
- Despite a 44 per cent increase since 2019 in the number of students registered by BACP as training to become therapists, demand for privately funded therapy is currently outstripping supply.[1] IFS professionals are even harder to find: the IFS Institute trained 5,000 people in 2025.[2]
- IFS therapy is not a magic bullet or cure-all, and will be offered and practised uniquely by each therapist – some of whom will fit well with your system, others may not.
- Timing matters. Maybe IFS as a first therapy is ideal; other systems might benefit from having had another form of therapy or inner practice previously.

What to look for in a therapist

As we know, everyone is different, there are no guarantees and, in the UK at least, therapy is a largely unregulated profession. Here are some ideas for your system to consider:

- Has the IFS professional received IFS therapy themselves and found it helpful?
- Are they a Certified IFS Therapist or Certified Practitioner? This means someone will have reviewed their IFS competence post-training.
- Are they willing to schedule a review early in your relationship to see how you are both experiencing the therapy?
- Are they qualified by education or experience if you require a specialist service?

Do they work relationally? Do you sense they value curiosity; can you sense their Self-energy and ability to lead their own system?

I'll leave you with a thought from the trauma therapist Bessel van der Kolk:

> The critical question is this: Do you feel that your therapist is curious to find out who *you* are and what *you*, not some generic 'PTSD patient', need? Are you just a list of symptoms ... or does your therapist take the time to find out why you do what you do and think what you think? Therapy is a collaborative process – a mutual exploration of your self. (2014, p. 212)

Notes

Introduction

1 World Health Organization (2022). *Mental Health*. Retrieved 6 March 2025 from <www.who.int/news-room/fact-sheets/detail/mental-health-strengthening-our-response>.
2 This statistic is taken from HM Treasury Public Expenditure Statistical Analyses 2022.
3 Here are links to the two directories featuring some of those who have undertaken training with the IFS Institute: <https://directory-uk.internalfamilysystemstraining.co.uk> and <https://ifs-institute.com/practitioners>.
4 An article on a pilot study has been published in the American Psychological Association's leading trauma specialty journal entitled: 'Online Group-Based Internal Family Systems Treatment for PTSD: Feasibility and Acceptability of Program for Alleviating and Resolving Trauma and Stress (PARTS)'. Details and links can be found here: <https://foundationifs.org/news/247-parts-pilot-study-published>.
5 For more on this, see Ecker et al. (2024), which features IFS.

Chapter 1

1 See <www.bacp.co.uk/news/news-from-bacp/2024/18-june-burst-the-self-doubt-campaign-launched-with-interactive-art-installation>.
2 Helen E. Lees (2023). The PARTS study: 'It is working ... that's starting to get people excited.' *PARTS&SELF*. <https://partsandself.org/the-parts-study-it-is-working-thats-starting-to-get-people-excited>.

Chapter 2

1 The idea of exiled parts may remind you of the Jungian terms 'shadow' or 'shadow self', which refer to parts of the personality that are 'buried' or 'hidden' from everyday consciousness. However, the terms are not synonymous, and the IFS concepts seem to me to be viewed less negatively. IFS and Jungian psychology engage therapeutically with what's out of awareness in very different ways. For more information: <https://www.thesap.org.uk/articles-on-jungian-psychology-2/about-analysis-and-therapy/the-shadow/>.

Chapter 3

1 For more on the difference between Self-energy in adults and children, read Martha Sweezy's blog in *Psychology Today*: <www.psychologytoday.com/gb/blog/internal-family-systems-therapy-for-shame-and-guilt/202501/ifs-therapy-aims-to-access-an>.

2 See note 2 Chapter 1

3 Schwartz, R. C. (n.d.). The Larger Self. IFS Institute. Retrieved from <www.ifs-institute.com/resources/articles/larger-self>.

4 Dubin, R., & Stewart, S. (2017). Checklist for noticing blending. Unpublished manuscript.

Chapter 4

1 For videos, podcasts and more, many of which feature Richard Schwartz doing IFS with interviewers and so on, visit the IFS Institute's YouTube channel. The video entitled 'IFS polarization demo' with Ty Cutner is especially popular.

2 For a thought-provoking and highly accessible article on consent, read Ash Chudgar (16 August 2023). Consent in IFS practice. *PARTS&SELF*. Retrieved from <https://partsandself.org/consent-in-ifs-practice>.

Chapter 5

1 Used slightly differently, the term 'loud empathy' is borrowed from child psychotherapist Dan Hughes's psychotherapy model PACE, more particularly from a webinar: 'Traumatised children: Why PACE heals (Play, Acceptance, Curiosity, Empathy)', which can be found at <https://www.childmentalhealthcentre.org/webinars/dr-dan-hughes>.

Chapter 7

1 For details of Ruth's workshops for both the public and professionals: <https://calmheart.co.uk>.

2 For more about Developmental Transformations: <www.developmentaltransformations.com/>.

Chapter 8

1 Gayle Williamson is a psychotherapist colleague and co-host of the podcast *Purely IFS with Emma and Gayle*. Its target audience is novice IFS professionals, but some of you may find something of interest. You can listen for free on our YouTube channel.

2 See The Conference Table strategy for helping polarized parts unblend at the same time in Sykes, C., Sweezy, M., & Schwartz, R. C. (2023). *Internal Family Systems Therapy for Addictions: Trauma-Informed, Compassion-Based Interventions for Substance Use, Eating, Gambling and More*. PESI Publishing.

Chapter 9

1 I recommend this online article about understanding IFS and adapting it for literal thinkers: <https://selfleadershipjourney.substack.com/p/using-ifs-for-literal-thinkers>.

Chapter 10

1 To read the rest of Holly Stoppit's blog (5 November 2024) Facilitating at the speed of fun, click: <www.hollystoppit.com/blog/facilitating-at-the-speed-of-fun>.

Chapter 11

1 Suicide statistics from the website of the charity Samaritans, whose volunteers answer a call for help every ten seconds: <https://www.samaritans.org/about-samaritans/research-policy/suicide-facts-and-figures/latest-suicide-data>.

Chapter 12

1 One of my responses to breast cancer was to meet with a nutritionist who helped me recognize that bodily feelings of fight-flight were being affected by how often I ate (and what) due to spikes and troughs in my blood glucose levels. My body tends to feel much calmer with gaps between meals. If you want to read more about flattening your glucose curve, I recommend Inchauspé, J. (2022). *Glucose Revolution: The Life-Changing Power of Balancing Your Blood Sugar.* Short Books.
2 Although not from an IFS lens, there is a helpful chapter on this in: Hughes, L. & Pengelly, P. (1997). *Staff Supervision in a Turbulent Environment: Managing Process and Task in Front-Line Services.* Jessica Kingsley.
3 For an IFS take on these two triangles, healthcare professionals and interested others can find for purchase recordings of a three-part workshop 'IFS and You: An IFS Take on the Drama Triangle and Healthy Triangle' here: <https://onlinevents.co.uk/presenter/emma-redfern>.

Chapter 13

1 To read the rest of Lara Eastburn's blog: <https://mailchi.mp/laraeastburn.com/one-word-authentic>.

Appendix 1

1 Inspired by The Self-Esteem Check-up by Positive Psychology.com, which can be found here: <https://positivepsychology.com>.

Appendix 2

1 That reference can be found here: <https://mft.nhs.uk/rmch/services/camhs/young-people/adverse-childhood-experiences-aces-and-attachment>.
2 For an illustrated introduction to IFS suitable for children and adults, see Cameron, D. (2009). *Why Did I Do That? How You Make Sense and Why There Is Hope.* Threshold Therapeutics Media.

Appendix 3

1 Statistics from an article in *The Guardian* by Jessica Bradley, 17 November 2024: <https://www.theguardian.com/society/2024/nov/17/real-nastiness-therapist-training-courses-in-uk-can-be-toxic-and-need-regulating-say-students>.

2 Details shared by Katie Nelson, CEO of the IFS Institute, as part of her opening remarks and welcome to the 2024 IFS Conference, which took place online.

References

Baden-Semper, L. (2024). Exploring ableism: Healing through self-connection and clarity. Conference presentation. 2024 IFS Annual Conference: IFS in evolution – broadening applications of the IFS model.

Chudgar, A. (2024). *A Year of Living Plurally.* <www.chudgar.com/tag/blog/>.

Culver, R. (2023). Embodied unblending: Drawing into Self. In Foot & Redfern 2023, pp. 226–8.

Ecker, B., Ticic, R., & Hulley, L. (2024). *Unlocking the Emotional Brain: Eliminating Symptoms at Their Roots Using Memory Reconsolidation.* Routledge.

Eastburn, L. (2023). Authentic. *ONE WORD: Re-examine the Language of Business and Marketing.* <https://mailchi.mp/laraeastburn.com/one-word-authentic>.

Foot, H. (2023). A new way of working in the business of health. In Foot & Redfern 2023, pp. 25–38.

Foot, H. & Redfern, E. E. (eds) (2023). *Freeing Self: IFS beyond the Therapy Room.* B.C. Allen Publishing and Tonic Books.

Karpman, S. (1968). Fairy tales and script drama analysis. *Transactional Analysis Bulletin, 7* (26), 39–43.

Khan, M. (2023). *Working within Diversity: A Reflective Guide to Anti-Oppressive Practice in Counselling and Therapy.* Jessica Kingsley Publishers.

Obama, M. (2018). *On Becoming Michelle.* Viking.

Perry, P. (2020). *The Book You Wish Your Parents Had Read (And Your Children Will be Glad That You Did).* Penguin Life.

Redfern, E. E. (2023a). *Internal Family Systems Therapy: Supervision and Consultation.* Routledge.

Redfern, E. E. (2023b). *Transitioning to Internal Family Systems Therapy: A Companion for Therapists and Practitioners.* Routledge.

Schmid, S. (2023). Becoming a therapist to children and young people. In Foot & Redfern (2023), (pp. 187–209).

Schwartz, R. C. & Sweezy, M. (2020). *Internal Family Systems Therapy,* 2nd edn. Guilford Press.

Sullivan, J., McVicker, S., Paisley, G., & Patton, P. (2023). Embodying IFS with native American clients: Composite Indigenous voices tell a story of IFS resonance. In J. Riemersma (ed.), *Altogether Us: Integrating the IFS Model with Key Modalities, Communities, and Trends.* Pivotal Press.

Sykes, C. (2017) An IFS lens on addiction: Compassion for extreme parts. In M. Sweezy & E. L. Ziskind (eds) *Innovations and Elaborations in Internal Family Systems Therapy* (pp. 29–48). Routledge.

Taussig, R. (2020). *Sitting Pretty: The View from My Ordinary Resilient Disabled Body.* HarperCollins.

Troughton, R. (2023). IFS – A physiotherapist's perspective. In Foot & Redfern, 2023, pp. 49–64.

Van der Kolk, B. (2014). *The Body Keeps the Score: Mind, Brain and Body in the Transformation of Trauma.* Penguin Books.

Vincentz, A. & Bubbers, J. (2023). Parenting from the inside. In Foot & Redfern, 2023, pp. 233–56.

Wildes, N. (2023). Heathens, heart tenders, and unwavering love: My journey with IFS and gender. In Foot & Redfern, 2023, pp. 141–59.

Acknowledgements

I wish to acknowledge and appreciate the founder of IFS, Richard C. Schwartz, and the other IFS trainers whose in-person IFSI training I have attended whether as student or program assistant: Frank Anderson, Osnat Arbel, Nick Austin, Barb Cargill, Mike Elkin, Paul Ginter, Susan McConnell, Mariel Pastor, Sue Smith. Thanks also to Ashley Curley and IFSI colleagues who organize the annual IFS conference and to colleagues I have had the pleasure of presenting and connecting with. Much appreciation also to Laura Wood who came to the UK to join with Naomi Nygaard and Martin Redfern to run an unforgettable weekend featuring IFS, parts and embodied approaches to eating disorders.

Likewise, I wish to honour members of the IFS UK community, past and present. These include the late Ginny Bennett, who with Nicola Hollings first brought Richard Schwartz to the UK; Irene Davies, who brought IFS to Broxbourne, near London, just as I found the confidence and desire to PA; and Nicola Hollings and Olivia Lester, who with Liz Calvert, Sue Smith and Krissy Tingle were at the helm of IFS UK in the early days.

I am grateful for the IFS UK monthly Friday morning Zoom meeting, Risa Adams's regular IFS peer drop-in, and the yearly Open Space event hosted by Liz Martins, Sarah Burns and Toni Buffham. Much appreciation to my long-time colleague and podcast co-host Gayle Williamson, to my co-editor Helen Foot, and to all those (trainers, consultants, supervisees, colleagues and clients) who have variously contributed to IFS books with my name on, published by Routledge and B.C. Allen Publishing and Tonic Books.

Appreciation and thanks to the team of friends and colleagues who read an early draft of this book and generously gave feedback: Sue Hunter, Bethany Parris, Graeme Smith, Samantha Tyler and Emma Wood. Special thanks to the following individuals for social media support as I've been 'putting myself out there': Karin Brauner (book ads, freebies and Onlinevents workshop collaborations), Rosie Parsons (photographer extraordinaire and founder of Slay Your Selfies), Julia Zatta (LinkedIn specialist), Samantha Tyler (who guided me on my lead magnet and subscriber newsletter) and Helen Walker (Visibility Queen and video expert). Thanks also to all those who are admins of and active in the myriad IFS Facebook groups – it's good to connect.

I extend gratitude to Victoria Roddam of Sheldon Press for taking a risk on me, and for her patience and curiosity. Appreciation also to Alisha Raj for her project management. Major thanks to highly experienced and skilled IFS and communication specialist Ash Chudgar who, with humanity and heart, clarified and strengthened my writing while preserving my distinctive voice and authorial intent – my parts are in awe. My mind and heart also turn to those with whom I previously worked at Hodder and Stoughton Ltd, an Hachette UK company. Special appreciation for the support, companionship and skills of colleague and neighbour Viv Wickham and the late Judy Adam.

More personally, I want to honour the skills and personal touch of nutritionist and gut health specialist Lesley Harper; specialist musculoskeletal physiotherapist Nigel Wilman; myofascial release, sports and remedial massage therapist and supporter Helen Watts; and Louise Stubbs of LMS Reflexology for foot and face reflexology (as well as the body lotions and potions).

I would like to honour my family and friends, especially my sister and her husband for the generous and heartfelt elder care they have provided over the years. Also, my husband Martin Redfern, a dramatherapist trained in IFS, as we reach the milestone of 25 years together as a married couple. Thanks, finally, to the Wednesday Club, who aid and abet our endeavours and help keep us real.

Last but by no means least, thanks go to you dear reader. Thank you for reading, exploring, dabbling (or is that paddling?) and engaging with this book in whatever ways feel appropriate to your system. I hope it felt like I held you in heart and mind as I wrote. Similarly, I trust my own voice came through; it should, because no generative artificial intelligence (AI) was used in the writing of this work. It's important to me that you know that. I value a person's (even a part's) ability to think for themselves and create uniquely (as much as that is possible considering none of us are likely to be blank slates). Also, I would prefer that no one use this publication to 'train' generative artificial intelligence (AI) technologies to generate text.

Index

Join the Sheldon Press community today, sign up for our newsletter!

- Select a **FREE eBook** or extract to read upon joining

- Keep up with our latest publishing and exciting author news

- Be the first to hear about book prize draws, free extracts, and upcoming author events

Simply scan the QR code below or head to www.sheldonpress.co.uk/newsletter to sign up.

RAISING READERS
Books Build Bright Futures

Dear Reader,

We'd love your attention for one more page to tell you about the crisis in children's reading, and what we can all do.

Studies have shown that reading for fun is the **single biggest predictor of a child's future life chances** – more than family circumstance, parents' educational background or income. It improves academic results, mental health, wealth, communication skills, ambition and happiness.[1]

The number of children reading for fun is in rapid decline. Young people have a lot of competition for their time. In 2024, 1 in 10 children and young people in the UK aged 5 to 18 did not own a single book at home.[2]

Hachette works extensively with schools, libraries and literacy charities, but here are some ways we can all raise more readers:

- Reading to children for just 10 minutes a day makes a difference
- Don't give up if children aren't regular readers – there will be books for them!
- Visit bookshops and libraries to get recommendations
- Encourage them to listen to audiobooks
- Support school libraries
- Give books as gifts

There's a lot more information about how to encourage children to read on our website: **www.RaisingReaders.co.uk**

Thank you for reading.

---

[1] OECD, '21st-Century Readers: Developing Literacy Skills in a Digital World', 2021, https://www.oecd.org/en/publications/21st-century-readers_a83d84cb-en.html

[2] National Literacy Trust, 'Book Ownership in 2024', November 2024, https://literacytrust.org.uk/research-services/research-reports/book-ownership-in-2024